YOU CAN CHANGE THE WORLD

Jill Johnstone

ZondervanPublishingHouse

Grand Rapids, Michigan

A Division of HarperCollinsPublishers

CONTENTS

INTRODUCTION

Did you know that there are about 230 different countries in our world? The people who live in them belong to many thousands of smaller groups who speak different languages, keep different customs, or originally came from different places.

We call these PEOPLE GROUPS, and the whole population of the world can be divided up into more than twelve thousand such groups. One PEOPLE GROUP you may have heard about is the Kurds. Although they do not have a country of their own (see page 50) they have their own language and customs and are very different from the other people among whom they live.

About this book
This book will tell you something about some COUNTRIES and PEOPLE GROUPS in the world where little is known about God's love shown to us in Jesus. It will help you to pray that this good news will become more widely known in these places.

There are twenty-six COUNTRIES and twenty-six PEOPLE GROUPS in this book, so if you look at one section a week it will last you for a whole year. These sections are also arranged in A-Z (alpha-betical) order, which will make them easier to find. So, the first week you can learn about the country of ALBANIA, the second week about a people group called the AZERIS, and so on.

You can read these sections alone, or with your family or friends. You could even start a "You Can Change the World" prayer club like some children living near me who helped me to put this book together.

At the end of each week's section there are seven prayers for you to pray for the COUNTRY or PEOPLE GROUP you have been learning about. You can pray them all at once, or better still, one on each day of the week.

Remember, all the stories and information, maps and flags, pictures and prayers are there to help you change the world by prayer! But perhaps you are wondering how that can really happen?

Changing the world
During winter a lot of snow falls in the mountains of Switzerland. When spring comes there is often a danger of avalanches. Sometimes avalanches have been started by a skier just shouting a few words. It only needs a small amount of snow to be disturbed by that shout, and soon thousands of tons of snow will be thundering down the mountainside.

In the same way a few words spoken to God our Father in Jesus' name can set off an "avalanche" of God's power in any part of the world. Even when we think our prayers are small and weak, God can use them if we trust in him, because he is so powerful.

Albania for instance
I started writing this book with the country of ALBANIA. The children in our "You Can Change the World" prayer club were sad because the Albanians were not allowed to worship God, to pray to him or have any books about him. They prayed hard for change in Albania, and soon the men who ruled Albania were removed from power.

Now people there are free to believe in Jesus. The children's prayers, and those of other Christians around the world, changed Albania, so I had to rewrite that chapter. Will your prayers help change other countries too?

Watch the TV news and look at newspapers for information about places and people in this book, and you will see answers to your prayers. The answers may not come right away, but we should never give up praying for the good things we know God wants to happen.

Is prayer important?
To help you pray, either for the things in this book or for your family or friends, here are some important things to remember. (If you find the Bible verses hard to understand, ask an older Christian to help you.)

• Prayer is simply talking with God. As we do this, we get to know him better, to understand his ways, to love him, and become his friends. When we pray we work together with God – and he wants to change the world!

• We don't have to shut our eyes and put our hands together and say special words for God to hear us, although sometimes this can help us to concentrate better. We can pray at any time and in any place by simply speaking to God quietly "in our heads."

• God knows everything, but we certainly don't. When we pray to him about something that troubles us we share with him in what he wants to do in that situation. Jesus talked to his special followers about this. Read what he said in John 15:14-15.

• Spiritual powers are trying to prevent God's will being done in the world. This is why sometimes we must keep on praying for a long time until our prayers are answered. Daniel discovered this for himself; read about it in Daniel 10:10-14. So, don't give up!

• Sometimes it is our own fault if our prayers are not being answered.

The problem might be
– our own selfishness (James 4:3)
– not being willing to say sorry to God, or to others, for things we have done wrong (Psalm 66:18; Matthew 5:23-24)
– ignoring the needs of someone we could help (Proverbs 21:13).

Finally, remember that the best way to learn more about prayer is to pray. I hope this book helps you to do that more and more, and that you will enjoy using it as much as I have enjoyed writing it. Let's change the world together through our prayers!

Jill Johnstone

To Help You

You will find the meaning of difficult words in this book in the word list on pages 118–119.

The main religions of the world besides Christianity are explained on pages 114–117.

On pages 124–125 I have listed some Christian organizations that can help you to learn more about the people you will be praying for, and on page 120 a few ideas to help you begin missionary work yourself.

ALBANIA

THE LAND THAT PRAYER CHANGED

Albanians sometimes call themselves "the eagle people." See the double-headed black eagle on their flag! Albania has beautiful scenery and wildlife. Oranges and olives grow on the hillsides but the people are very poor. The shelves of shops are bare and one child in three goes hungry. Wooden carts are used on farms. Even in Tirana, the capital, you can see donkeys, carts, and bicycles but very few motor vehicles.

Hospitals have little modern equipment and few medicines. The orphanages are very crowded because many people have large families and cannot afford to keep all their children at home. There are not enough orphanage staff to look after them, so babies are left in their cots all day while children in poor clothing huddle together in crowded rooms with no toys or games to play with.

Cut off!

Christians from other European countries have sent truckloads of supplies to Albania. But the people are so desperate for food that some have attacked the trucks and stolen the supplies, so they don't reach those most needing the help. Why is this land in such a sorry state?

These problems arose because in 1944 Albania became a Communist country. Enver Hoxha ruled for the next forty-one years and isolated Albania from the rest of the world. Albanians had to do without modern goods and manage with the minimum of food and supplies. Christian and Muslim books and meetings, and even Christian and Muslim first names were banned. Parents were forbidden to teach their own children about Jesus, and it was against the law to pray! Christians in other countries wondered how they could get the message of Jesus into such a difficult country.

When I started writing this book it was almost impossible to get even one Bible into Albania. Several children in our "You Can Change the World" club began to pray regularly for Albania. They believe that their prayers, with those of other Christians, have changed the situation there.

New hope

In 1991 the Communist government fell from power and a new government was formed which allows Christians and Muslims to worship and speak about their beliefs. Since then several Christian groups from other parts of Europe have held meetings in homes, public buildings, and in the streets. Some Albanians have become Christians. Several hundreds have been baptized, and churches have been started.

Before the Communists came to power Albania was the only Muslim country in Europe. Now Muslims from other countries are working hard to make it a Muslim country once again.

Albanians are showing that they want more than food and clothes. A Christian paper called SOON,* written in easy English which some

A

is for Albania, where Christians were banned; But God has stepped in and is changing this land.

Albanians can understand, was sent into Albania. It has true stories about people who have found peace and joy in Jesus. More than ten thousand Albanians who want to hear all they can about Jesus and the Bible have written asking for SOON to be sent regularly.

You can pray for Albania

1 Dear Lord Jesus, please provide the money for SOON to be sent regularly to the Albanians who have asked for it.

2 Help those who read SOON to realize what wonderful things you can do in their lives too.

3 Use radio broadcasts to make your good news clear to those who listen, so that they too may come to know you.

4 Help those Albanians who have recently come to know you for themselves to learn more about you and tell others about their faith.

5 Encourage Christians around the world to pray for Albania and to send them Bibles and Christian books.

6 Help people taking food, clothes, and medicines to Albania to reach those who need them most.

7 Help boys and girls in Albania who were born on my birthday to hear about you, and come to trust you.

Crowds tear down a statue of the Communist ruler Enver Hoxha.

AZERIS

GUARDIANS OF FIRE

Farzali lives in a city called Baku, the capital of Azerbaijan, a republic of the old Soviet Union.* His people, the Azeris, are Muslims who have been fighting against another people group living in Azerbaijan called the Armenians, who have a Christian background.

Farzali was at school when his friend Babeli asked him, "Will you come to my house after school?"

"Sorry, I can't," Farzali

> **A**zeris, fire guardians of Azerbaijan; They long to be holy, but don't know God's plan.

grumbled. "Since the fighting with the Armenians, my mother won't let me go anywhere unless my big brother is with me."

Babeli nodded. "My mother's as bad. She was terrified when our people dragged Armenians from their houses and killed them. We had some Armenian friends, but now it's dangerous even to speak to them."

"There aren't many Armenians still here. Our friend Samweli and his family went to the Armenian Republic last year."

"I remember him. I went to his house but my mother didn't like it. She said the Armenians would try to make me a Christian."

Farzali looked horrified. "That would be terrible. My grandfather says it's unforgivable for an Azeri to become a Christian."

Are we Muslims?

As the teacher came in, Babeli whispered, "Why do they make such a fuss? My family doesn't go to the mosque, although we say we're Muslims."

Farzali's thoughts wandered from the lesson. Were his family Muslims or not? His great-grandfather certainly was; Farzali's brother read the Koran to him each evening, but his father never read it.

The next day Farzali's father called him. "Farzali, on Saturday we are taking great-grandfather to visit your uncle on the farm."

Clean and pure

Azeris want to be made clean and pure, but neither fire worship nor Islam can do that for them – only Jesus can. Few Azeri people have heard the truth about the Lord Jesus, but now the New Testament and a children's Bible have been printed in their language, and some Christian radio programs have been made. So now is the time to pray that Farzali and his people may be willing to listen to the message of Jesus and believe in him.

"Oh good," smiled Farzali. He loved his great-grandfather who was still strong, although over one hundred years old. Many Azeris live long lives!

As Farzali's uncle showed them around his vineyard he said, "Today is a special feast when we speak with our ancestors and bathe in the river that flows from the mountains. When our people became Muslims many centuries ago only a few went on worshiping our ancestors and fire, but we like to keep some ceremonies from the past."

Farzali bathed in the river. Even great-grandfather carefully lowered himself into the water. Farzali felt fresh and glowing. *Was he really in touch with his ancestors?* he wondered.

The ancient Greeks called the Azeris "fire guardians" because the Azeris worshiped fire, believing it to be the purest and holiest symbol. Farzali's cousin wore a red dress on her wedding day as a symbol of fire. Farzali was wondering, *Which is true: the old Azeri religion, or Islam, or the*

Christian religion which the Armenians believe?

* The old Soviet Union, or USSR (Union of Soviet Socialist Republics), is today called the CIS (Commonwealth of Independent States).

You can pray for the Azeris

1 Lord Jesus, please stop the fighting between Azeris and Armenians. Comfort those whose loved ones have been killed.

2 Send Christians to Azerbaijan to teach what the Bible says. Help other Christians who live there to tell Azeris about Jesus too.

3 Please may the New Testament and children's Bible be given to those Azeris who will read them.

4 Teach Azeri people that Jesus can give them the holiness and purity they want so much.

5 Help the Christians planning Azeri radio programs to make them interesting and answer the questions Azeri people have about Jesus.

6 Help Azeri children to understand that you are God and that Jesus is your Son.

7 You promised that there will be people from every language, nation, and tribe in heaven. Please bring Azeris to believe in Jesus.

BHUTAN

LAND OF THE THUNDER DRAGON

"Why is there a roaring dragon on our flag?" asked Sungay.

"Hush dear, it's the Thunder Dragon. Haven't you heard him roar when there's a storm? It's all part of our religion."

Sungay felt scared as he watched the monks dancing in their ugly masks at the Buddhist festival.

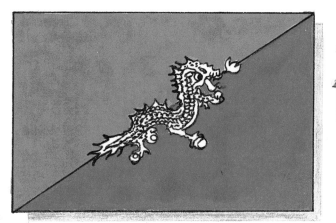

Highest mountains
Sungay lives in Bhutan, a small country between China and India in the eastern Himalayas. These are the highest mountains in the world, with many beautiful forests and powerful rivers. There are even bears in these forests!

Sungay's parents are farmers, with five goats which is all anyone is allowed to keep. Too many goats would destroy the trees and grass. Sungay would like to go to school with his brother, but only one child in four starts school and many soon leave. As

a result only one person in twenty can read. Doctors and dentists are very scarce too, and many people have health problems.

In Bhutan some men have several wives and some women have several husbands , which seems very strange to us

because it is against God's law. One husband may be a village head-man, often away from home; the second husband may barter cheese and butter for wheat, rice, and chilies. The third one might look after the sheep and yaks, and the fourth sees to the farm produce. A man with a lot of land may have one wife to look after the household, another to work in the fields, and another to care for the cattle.

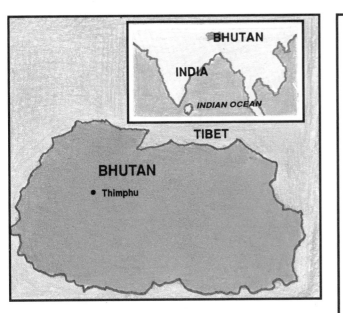

Preaching Illegal

When a factory is opened or when officials are appointed, a Buddhist religious ceremony is held. Christians don't like to take part in these. Once the mayor of Thimphu lost his job because of his Christian activities. It is illegal to preach anything except Buddhism (see page 115) in Bhutan. People may not even hold Christian meetings in their homes.

Only about ten truly Bhutanese people are Christians, though there are a few Christians from nearby India and Nepal living in Bhutan. However, Christians from other countries are allowed into Bhutan to help with health care, farming, and training.

Luck and the king

Bhutan's king, Jigme Singya Wangchuck, was married to four sisters on the same day! Astrologers, men who think they can tell the future from the stars, had to find a lucky day for the wedding. The king's subjects can visit him whenever they wish and about thirty go each day. The king wears national dress, the *kho*, a simple knee-length tunic. His people must also wear the *kho* whenever they leave the house.

Thimphu, the capital city, has few paved roads. There are more mules, cows, and horses in the streets than cars. Bhutan has only one car to every 250 people; while in England there is one to every three. The big houses have beautifully carved woodwork and painted walls. Many people are poor and children have neither toys nor books. They eat rice with hot peppers or chilies three times a day.

King Jigme Singya Wangchuck.

You can pray for Bhutan

1 Lord Jesus, please send Christian teachers, farmers, medical workers, and engineers to Bhutan.

2 Help the workers of the Leprosy Mission, Interserve, and Santal Mission to show your love to sick people.

3 Help the few Bhutanese Christians not to be afraid of Buddhism, but to know you are Almighty.

4 Give Christians courage, love, and power to share their faith in you.

5 Help Christians to make radio programs that can be broadcast into Bhutan.

6 Help the Christians to give gospel records to Buddhists so they may hear God's Word.

7 May your Holy Spirit work throughout Bhutan, so that those who hear about God will believe in you.

BALUCH

CARPET WEAVERS OF PAKISTAN

Sadar tossed the freshly cut wheat onto the bullock cart. "Not a bad harvest this year," he thought.

His grandfather, with his white beard, turban, and his long homespun shirt over baggy trousers, was glad of Sadar's help. He could not manage the small farm without him.

When his father and brother Ghaus went to the city of Karachi (the capital of Pakistan) to find work, Sadar became responsible for much of the farm work although he was not yet thirteen. It was difficult work, because of the fierce heat in summer and bitter cold in winter.

The old bullock lumbered into the high-walled courtyard leading to the breeze-block house built by Sadar's father. This house was much better than the reed shack in which they had once lived, or the goat-hair tent of which grandfather spoke!

Sadar's sisters were weaving at the carpet looms where they spent most of the day. To make the beautiful designs passed down through the family for generations means they must tie thousands of tiny knots. When he smelt the *nan* (wheat bread) and curry his mother was preparing for the evening meal, Sadar realized how hungry he was.

Meanwhile, in Karachi, his brother Ghaus lay half-unconscious in the gutter. Their father hadn't seen him for months, but didn't want the rest of the family to know. Every day,

as soon as he finished work on his street kebab stall, he went looking for his son. Ghaus was taking drugs like thousands of other young people and his father was afraid that by the time he was found it might be too late to save him.

A rich province

Sadar's farm is in Baluchistan, one of Pakistan's four provinces. Baluchistan has natural gas, copper, iron ore and coal, and plenty of fish in the southern sea, but the Baluch people feel they are neglected by the Pakistan government.

B

for Baluch, who fish, herd, and trade
In the lands where beautiful carpets are made.

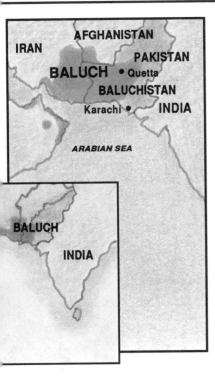

A needy people

Most Baluch cannot read, but they like to listen to programs in their own Baluch language from Radio Quetta (the capital of Baluchistan) and other countries nearby. Many of the five million Baluch have left the country areas to find work in the city of Karachi or overseas in the Gulf states.

Students who listen to foreign radio programs lead the struggle for Baluchistan to be independent. They complain that most of their natural gas is used in Pakistan's other provinces. They badly need better roads and railways, development of water supplies, health care, and adequate schools.

The whole of Pakistan is strongly Muslim. It is almost impossible for Christians to go into Baluchistan to preach about Jesus, but about fifteen young Baluch men have become Christians. Loving Christians find that when they explain the Word of God to their Baluch friends, they listen. A new translation of the New Testament in Baluchi is being prepared, and some Christian tapes are available.

How can Christians help the Baluch? They need jobs, health care, and reading lessons. Christians can show Jesus' love by meeting these needs. When some sick Baluch were prayed for in Jesus' name, they were healed. This showed them that Jesus is all-powerful, and they turned to him for forgiveness.

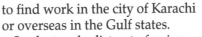

You can pray for the Baluch

1 Dear Lord, please bring whole Baluch families and villages to faith in Jesus – women and girls as well as men and boys.

2 Show yourself to the Baluch people in dreams and visions and in healing power so that they may know that you are the true God.

3 Send Christians to tell drug addicts in Karachi that Jesus can set them free from wanting to take drugs and can give them a new life.

4 Send Christians to provide work and health care and to meet the other needs of the Baluch people.

5 Help Christians to find a way to broadcast your message to the Baluch in their own language.

6 Help the few Baluch Christians to tell others what Jesus has done for them.

7 Make it possible for Christian missionaries to go to Baluchistan, and to tell the Baluch people your good news.

CHAD

WHERE THE LAKE IS DRYING UP

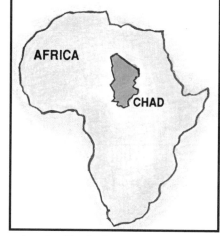

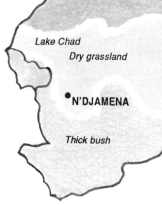

CHAD

Sand dunes

Lake Chad
Dry grassland

•N'DJAMENA

Thick bush

Three parts

Like its flag, Chad is divided into three parts: the north is sand dunes, the central part dry grassland, and the south thick bush. As Chad is in the center of Africa and hundreds of miles from the sea, it is difficult for goods from overseas to be taken there. This fact, plus frequent wars, lack of rain, and infertile soil make Chad one of the world's poorest countries.

Lake Chad, in the southwest, was once huge and many fish could be caught there. Cattle herders with their oxen were able to move from island to island. Farmers cultivated the small patches of fertile land which were left when the lake evaporated in the dry season. Today, because so many people and cattle are using the lake, it is drying up.

Some people grumble about the rain, but they wouldn't if they lived in Chad. Rain brings little children running naked into the streets, laughing and splashing in the puddles. Frogs emerge and catch termites. The people catch them too – they taste good fried!

More than one hundred languages are spoken in Chad, the main ones being French and Chad Arabic. The people belong to many different tribes and religions and often fight. After years of civil war the country is now under the control of the president, Idriss Deby.

C

stands for Chad where there's so little rain; The people and cattle are hungry for grain.

What they believe

The religion of the north and central part of Chad is Islam, mixed with animism. Animists believe that trees, rocks, and animals contain living spirits.

Both animists and Muslims wear charms round their necks, hoping for protection from illness, curses, or other troubles. These charms are little bags containing bits of bark, hair, cattle horn, or other "magic" things, put in them by the local healer. Muslims also wear charms with verses from the Koran inside.

When people become Christians they burn their charms. They know that Jesus is stronger than any other power and they need not be afraid any more. Most Christians live in the south, where the people are very different from the northern Muslims and speak different languages.

Mission to Chad

Daniel and Joanna live in Chad with their missionary parents. They have lessons at home as there are no English-speaking schools. They would like more friends because some local children punch them and throw stones. They enjoy seeing camels and donkeys, but do not like the mosquitoes and sandstorms. Their parents give Christian cassettes and booklets to their visitors and make friends with Muslims at the mosque and in the market.

Some of their missionary friends work in an orphan-age; others live far from the town and must cross a river by canoe to reach their village. They are translating the Bible and giving medical care to the villagers. Missionaries must learn two languages, often three; first French, then Chad Arabic, which is used in offices and shops, and then the language of the people they work with.

Many of these local languages have never been written down, so there are no books to learn from. About 74 people groups have no part of the Bible in their own language and no Christian or missionary living among them. How would you have learned about Jesus if there were no Christians who spoke your language?

You can pray for Chad

1 Lord Jesus, please send enough rain for the crops to grow well in Chad this year.

2 Send missionaries to translate the Bible into the languages of every people group in Chad.

3 Help missionaries who live in the villages to learn the languages well so they can tell people about you.

4 Send loving Christians to give medical care and to help in farming the land.

5 Help people to put their trust in you and not in charms.

6 Make Muslims eager to listen to the cassettes about the Bible and read the booklets that the missionaries give them.

7 Help missionaries' children to be happy in Chad and to keep well and strong.

CHILDREN OF THE STREETS

IN SOUTH AMERICA

COLOMBIA
• Bogota

ECUADOR

BRAZIL

PERU
• Lima

Rio de Janeiro •

SOUTH AMERICA

A nasty surprise

Chico smiled at the well-dressed lady: "I'm so sorry I bumped you."

"That's all right," she replied, fondling his black curly hair. Chico disappeared like a rocket into the side streets of Rio de Janeiro, laughing to himself. He'd had a good day; a radio from a parked car, breakfast from a fruit trolley, and now a nice fat purse from the unsuspecting lady. For a few hours at least life seemed good to Chico from Brazil, one of the world's thirty million street children.

Joining a gang

Pedro's parents were both killed in Peru's guerilla war which flared up in 1982. He, his brother Pancho, and sister Karen went to find food and work in Lima, the capital; amazingly they are still alive and still together. Pancho is deaf, but makes a little money as a shoe-shine boy. Pedro and Karen belong to a gang. They fight for food and sniff paint thinner, which makes them sleepy and drugged.

Helping the homeless

All over South America millions of children live on the streets. Most are dirty and difficult to help. The police often beat and even shoot them. They are a problem because they soon learn to steal, fight, use drugs, and even kill. Sleeping in railway stations, shop doorways, and cardboard boxes, many still say life is better than at home with drunken parents or constant hunger.

In Lima, Scripture Union workers take such children to their camps, play soccer and sing with them, and provide food. Some children have become Christians. Workers from missions like World Vision run orphanages, farms, hostels, feeding programs and training schemes.

Señor Jaramillo, a rich businessman in Bogota, Colombia, saw a little street girl knocked down and killed while she ran to pick up an empty box. It changed his life. Each night he goes down into the sewers searching for homeless children who live there. He wears scuba-diving gear because the torrents of water after heavy rainfalls could drown him. He gives food,

C for the children whose home is the street,
Who long for warm clothes and a dinner to eat.

clothes, education, and jobs to as many as he can.

Over a hundred years ago, thousands of children slept on the streets of London and other British cities. Dr. Barnardo and George Müller of Bristol, both Christians, opened homes for them. They trusted God for the money to feed and clothe the children: he never failed them.

In South America there is an urgent need for Christians to take orphaned and unwanted children into their homes, or create places of safety and shelter for them. Some government orphanages exist, but cannot provide the healing love of Jesus that these hurt, lonely children need.

As you pray for these children, many of them your own age, remember to thank God for your home and family, food and clothes.

You can pray for the street children

1 Dear Lord, please show South American Christians that they need to care for the many children running wild in their cities.

2 Provide men with faith and concern, like Dr. Barnardo, to open homes for children in South America.

3 Help Christians to give money to provide food and shelter for street children.

4 Help every child in projects run by World Vision and other missions to know and understand your love.

5 Send Christians filled with your Holy Spirit to lead hundreds of these children to faith in you.

6 Bless Scripture Union camps in Lima, Peru. May Christians give enough money for these camps to continue.

7 Show us, Lord, what we can do to help children in need in our own country.

DJIBOUTI

WHERE MEN CHEW LEAVES LIKE CATERPILLARS

AFRICA

DJIBOUTI

The flight to Djibouti was delayed and the heat made everybody irritable. "I won't take off! The plane is overloaded!" shouted the pilot. "We'll never clear the mountain."

"How can we be overloaded?" asked a man. "DC9s hold seventy-two passengers and there are only forty of us."

"We're overloaded with eight and a half tons of *khat*, but if we refuse to take it . . . !" The flight attendant drew her finger across her throat. (*Khat* is a leaf which, when chewed, makes people dreamy and thin. *Khat* is big business in Djibouti, much more valuable than airline passengers!)

The *khat* traders scowled fiercely, their daggers poking from their belts. The flight finally departed, leaving behind two large Somali ladies and some luggage.

The plane just cleared the mountain at the end of the runway. At Djibouti's main airport, after the plane landed, crowds of traders and buyers jostled, desperate for *khat*. Cheeks soon bulged as with sleepy satisfaction men made off home with their supplies.

Boomerang-shaped

Djibouti is a small boomerang-shaped African country, between Ethiopia and Somalia. Peter lives in the capital, Djibouti Town, with his missionary parents. It was too hot to sleep. His mosquito net had come untucked and mosquitoes zoomed in. Anyway, noise from crickets, cats, dogs, and roosters made sleep impossible.

Soon Peter heard the neighbor sweeping her

yard, then the clang of her washing bowl. He imagined her rubbing fiercely at the stained clothes. Peter got up; that day he was going by bus with his father to Yoboki.

Bus journeys in Djibouti are fun, if you don't mind waiting ages until the bus is full. Chickens lie with their feet tied together; bowls of clothes or *khat* and bags of rice or corn fill the aisles. Goats and roosters travel on the roof. Travelers may see some of the wild animals of Djibouti.

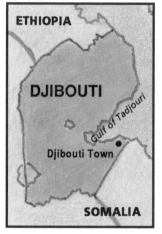

ETHIOPIA

DJIBOUTI

Gulf of Tadjouri

Djibouti Town

SOMALIA

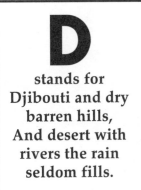

D

stands for Djibouti and dry barren hills, And desert with rivers the rain seldom fills.

Digging wells

Peter loves traveling with his dad, visiting the nurses who vaccinate babies and teach local midwives. Yoboki is his favorite place. Once the whole valley was just miles of sand. Then lady missionaries dug wells there. At first the people thought they were crazy, but now that the mission-aries have planted gardens, and the sandy valley is green with crops, they understand.

Once Peter took the ferry across the gulf of Tadjoura. His father was taking supplies to mid-wives working among the Afar people. A kind Afar lady invited them into her *ari* – a hut made of branches covered by skins and waterproof mats. Afars are tall slender people whose villages are built near water, where they find grazing for their camels, goats, cows, sheep, horses, and donkeys.

About as many Somalis as Afars live in Djibouti. Somalis, like Afars, are Muslims and their way of life is similar. Few Afars and only a small number of Somalis are Christians. A Muslim who becomes a Christian will be persecuted.

Both groups like to learn, so missionaries in Djibouti Town teach them English and French. Classes are held in the Christian book-

store. Men sit reading Christian literature. There are early-reading books in Afar and talks and songs on cassettes. Do you sing songs that are actual words from the Bible? It is very good to have songs like that in Afar and Somali so that people who cannot read, can still learn God's word.

You can pray for Djibouti

1 Lord Jesus, please help the missionaries in the clinics and villages to tell people about Jesus.

2 Make the gardens and crops grow well so that there is enough food to eat.

3 Open the hearts of the people in Djibouti to hear your Word.

4 Help people remember Bible songs, so that your truth goes into their minds and hearts.

5 May both Afar and Somali people come to know you.

6 Help those who make cassettes and write books to tell the truth about you clearly.

7 Bring people into the bookstore to buy and read Christian books.

DOGON

PEOPLE WITH A FIVE-DAY WEEK

AFRICA

Oumar climbs to the caves

Swinging dangerously on a rope, Oumar climbed hundreds of feet to reach caves hollowed out of the cliff. He was collecting pigeon dung to sell as fertilizer at the market. The Dogon have few fields in their villages in Mali, central Africa, so fertilizer helps them to make the most of those they have. Beyond their villages a dry plain borders the Sahara Desert where nothing grows, so every foot of soil is precious. They even hoist their dead up the cliffs on ropes and bury them in the caves!

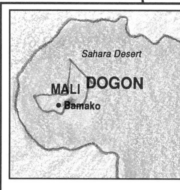

Sahara Desert

MALI **DOGON**

• Bamako

D stands for Dogon who climb very high
To caves in the cliffs, far in the sky.

Dogon life

Dogon life is full of ceremony. The people love to dance on brightly colored stilts wearing cowrie shell and hibiscus masks, and unlike most of the world they have a five-day week.

The strong tribal beliefs of the Dogon made it difficult to interest them in the message of Jesus, but there are things that have helped them to understand God's ways and believe in him.

Praying for rain

Rain is vital for the crops, and one year, despite all the sacrifices of the spirit worshipers and chanting of Muslims in the streets, rain did not come. In one village a visitor told the elders, "In my village I've seen that when Christians pray their God answers. Ask the Christians. I'm sure their God will send rain." Rather reluctantly the elders consulted the Christians.

"We will pray," the Christians replied, "but only if all sacrifices to the spirits and all Muslim prayers stop. Then when rain comes everybody will know that our God sent it." The leaders agreed, so the Christians prayed and rain fell.

At once the spirit worshipers ran out to make sacrifices and the Muslims started to pray. This stopped the rain. "You broke your promise not to pray!" the visitor scolded. "Apologize to the Christians and ask them to pray again."

"We are sorry," the elders said. "Please pray again. Our crops are dying, and we will all be hungry." God lovingly sent plenty of rain in answer to the Christians' prayers, so the Dogon know that the Christian God answers prayer.

Punishment

If a Dogon person does something wrong the elders may make him or her leave the village. This is a dreadful punishment because afterwards they have to make a new start in life on their own.

If, however, they confess to having done wrong and ask forgiveness, they must bring a goat or sheep to the edge of the village.

The elders kill the animal, and make a trail of blood from the place of sacrifice to the door of the wrongdoer's home. Then they are once again fully accepted by the village. Christians explain how sin makes us unfit to be in heaven, but the sacrifice of Jesus, the Lamb of God, makes us acceptable to God the Father, if we believe in him and are truly sorry for doing wrong.

Among the half million Dogon about one in a hundred is a Christian. Some Dogon are Muslims but most are animists.* Dogon Christians would like a Bible school to train pastors but the missionaries first want to translate the whole Bible into the Dogon language. Many listen to God's word on Christian radio programs.

* See page 114.

You can pray for the Dogon

1 Dear Lord, please help Dogon Christians explain to their friends about forgiveness through your sacrifice on the cross.

2 Help those working on the Dogon Bible to translate it clearly and accurately.

3 Help missionaries to teach Dogon pastors and to open a Bible school for them.

4 Free those whose lives are controlled by fear of the spirits so they can know and worship you.

5 Send needed rain, so that the people may have crops both for themselves and to sell to others.

6 Thank you that some Dogon customs and sacrifices help them to understand about Jesus' dying for them.

7 Help missionaries and Dogon Christians to teach children the truth of your Word and to bring many to believe in you.

ETHIOPIA

LAND OF REFUGEES AND SINGING CHRISTIANS

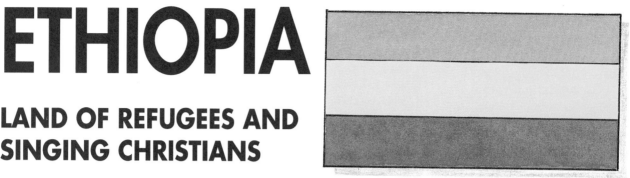

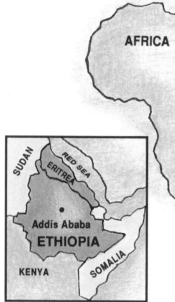

Jal, a nine-year-old boy, lives in a refugee camp. "When soldiers came to my village I ran away with five of my friends. We walked and walked, looking for our families but were afraid to shout because of the soldiers. We feared the big sickness [typhoid] and the flooded rivers. I tried to catch some fish but the crocodiles scared me, so we only had roots and leaves to eat. One day some villagers said, 'You're not in Sudan anymore, you're in Ethiopia,' and they sent us to this place."

Jal dreams of . . . good food . . . clothes . . . shoes to stop "chiggers" (itchy insects) burrowing into his toes . . . and a home with his parents again.

E

for Ethiopia, where famine is rife; Where fighting and hunger took many a life.

Singing Christians!

Mengistu's government imprisoned Christian leaders and closed churches. In spite of this the churches grew and now thousands of Ethiopians know Jesus personally. Oh how they sing! They sing going along the road to market or washing their clothes by the river, and wherever they go they tell others what Jesus has done for them.

After years when no church services could be held, returning missionaries tell of ten thousand people who came to hear them preach, listening for six hours in the pouring rain. Some even slept out in the rain so they could listen again the

next day. The missionaries were amazed to hear them singing, as only Africans can sing. There are about seventy-five Bible schools for training pastors and evangelists. That may sound like a lot, but the forty-nine million Ethiopians speak more than 120 languages. About one in three Ethiopians is a Muslim. Many have not yet heard about Jesus.

One Ethiopian language is Afar, which is also spoken in Djibouti (see page 20). They have a proverb which says, "It's the camel at the front who refuses to go, but it's the camel at the back who gets the beating!"

In Sadik's camp

You have probably seen pictures on TV of the famine in Ethiopia and the refugee camps. Jal's camp is only one of many. Sadik, who is also nine, lies on a bed in an open-air hospital in another refugee camp. Civil war in the neighboring country of Somalia, in which thousands of ordinary people have been killed, forced his family to leave the capital Mogadishu.

"In Mogadishu we had a lovely home. We even had a TV and video. Here we are lucky to get food. I'm afraid the water will run out. In the daytime it's hot but the nights are freezing."

Besides the refugees from Sudan and Somalia, there

are also Ethiopians who fled the civil war in their own country.

Since the overthrow of Mengistu, the former Communist dictator, many have returned. There are 300,000 soldiers of the previous government in

refugee camps too, some only boys of thirteen. They fear they will be killed if they return home.

The war left Ethiopia's villages empty, buildings and crops destroyed, ports bombed, and no police force to control violence. The new government has much to do to get the country running smoothly.

You can pray for Ethiopia

1 Lord Jesus, please help Ethiopian Christians to trust in you even when they are hungry and suffering.

2 Send Christians to care for the many refugees and to show them your love. Make it possible for them to go back to their own villages and families.

3 Let the joyful witness of the Christians bring Communists and Muslims to have faith in you.

4 May the students in the Bible schools have the food, clothes, and money that they need.

5 Use radio broadcasts to reach people who are in misery and fear, that they may turn to you and find help and peace.

6 Help those who are translating the Bible into the different Ethiopian languages.

7 Encourage Ethiopian Christians to work among refugee children, and give them your love for them.

EUSKALDUNAK

NEITHER SLAVES NOR TYRANTS

The Basque people, whose name means "people of the wastelands," call themselves Euskaldunak, "people on the same side." Independent, hardworking and proud, they have a motto that they will be "neither slave nor tyrant" – that is, they won't be oppressed by anyone, but neither will they oppress others.

Living in southwest France and northeast Spain, many Basques want their own country. Although the Spanish government gave them home rule in 1980, not everyone was satisfied. One Basque terrorist group called ETA has killed over six hundred people by bombing and shooting.

Basques were some of the first sailors to brave the seas in small boats to catch whales, and the first man to sail around the world was a Basque. Every year they have a rowing race in the stormy Bay of Biscay.

The Basques are strong and good at sports. They enjoy weightlifting, wood-chopping competitions, and their own game, pelota, played with a small goatskin ball thrown hard against a wall from a long curved basket. It is said to be the fastest ball game in the world and was recently included in the Olympic Games.

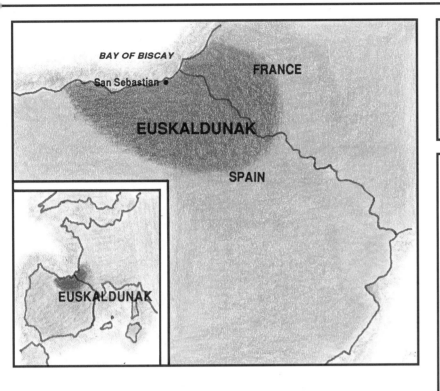

BAY OF BISCAY

San Sebastian

FRANCE

EUSKALDUNAK

SPAIN

EUSKALDUNAK

Basques are strongly Roman Catholic, and there is no Basque-speaking evangelical church to share the truth about new life in Jesus. A few Basques trusted Jesus when some young missionaries preached to them in the open air. Some Basques listen to Christian radio programs, and others are studying the Bible with missionaries or by mail.

You can pray for the Basques

1 Dear Lord, please help families hurt in terrorist attacks to forgive and not to grow bitter.

2 Help missionaries learning the difficult Basque language to be determined to get it right.

3 Help each Basque person studying the Bible by mail or in groups to understand your truth.

4 Give your Holy Spirit to those who plan, produce, and broadcast Christian radio programs in Basque.

5 Prepare the minds of those who listen to the radio broadcasts to understand what you have done for them.

6 Give missionaries opportunities to show God's love and friendship to the people they meet.

7 Help Basque believers to share their faith and start a Basque-speaking church where whole families can worship you together.

Ignatius of Loyola

Ignatius was sitting with his grandfather around the warm kitchen stove in his parents' large farmhouse. "Tell me about Ignatius of Loyola," he begged. He knew Grandpa loved to tell this story!

"Over four hundred years ago there was a rich Basque nobleman, a brave soldier. One day he was badly wounded and while recovering he read lots of books about Jesus and the saints. He thought, *It is better to be a soldier for Jesus than a soldier of this world.* He gave away all his money and began telling others about Jesus. He started a missionary society called the Jesuits and when he died there were more than one thousand Jesuits serving God all over the world."

"Tell me about him going to prison," pleaded Ignatius. "Why did the people put him there?"

"Often good men are punished," Grandpa said sadly. "Church leaders didn't like the way he preached so they imprisoned him for two years. But other brave men followed him. One was Francis Xavier who went

to many countries, especially India, bringing people to faith in Christ."

You may like to pray this well-known prayer of Ignatius of Loyola:
Teach us, good Lord, to serve you as you deserve;
to give and not to count the cost;
to fight and not to heed the wounds;
to toil and not to seek for rest;
to labor and not to ask for any reward
save [except] that of knowing that we do your will.

FIJI

LAND OF 300 ISLANDS

The beautiful islands of Fiji, with their warm sunny beaches, lie in the Pacific Ocean; if you look carefully at the world map (on page 64) you will find them to the east of Australia.

The shield on the flag is from the coat of arms of Fiji. At the top a lion holds a cocoa pod. In the shield's four sections are sugarcane, a coconut palm, a bunch of bananas, and the dove of peace. Sugar, and copra from the coconut palm are two of Fiji's main exports.

The symbol of Christianity in Fiji is a deep-sea canoe. These are different from the canoes paddled in the rivers and coral reefs around the island. They are built to go far from the shore to other islands. Fijian Christians believe the love of Jesus is too wonderful to keep to themselves, so they use the picture of a deep-sea canoe to show they must share his love on other islands too. In the 1800s many Fijians died taking the good news of Jesus to other Pacific islands.

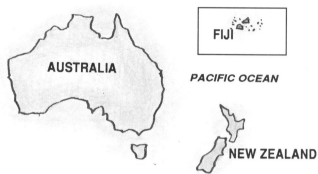

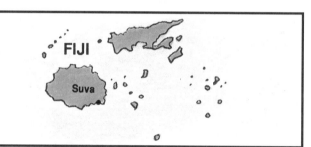

F

stands for Fiji with hundreds of isles, The climate is sunshine and so are the smiles.

28

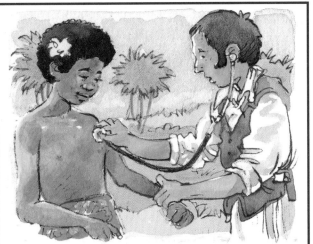

"Who will go?"

Many years ago Dr. Brown, a missionary, wanted Fijian evangelists to go with him to the land of Papua New Guinea (see page 70). When Dr. Brown asked for volunteers at the pastors' training college he thought no one would be willing to go, because forty thousand people in Fiji had just died from measles. How could they leave Fiji now? To his amazement all eighty-four students said they would go with him! One of their leaders stood up and said, "Our minds are made up; we have given ourselves to God's work. If we live we live. If we die we die."

(see page 70)

You can pray for Fiji

1 Lord Jesus, please give the Christians in Fiji hearts full of love for you and for other people.

2 Help Fijians remember that your truth is not to be kept for themselves but to be shared with other people.

3 Help the Fijians to be sorry for the way they have treated the Muslims, Hindus, and Sikhs.

4 Send Christians full of love and the power of your Holy Spirit to show care and concern for the Indian people.

5 Help real Christians to share your love with their neighbors and friends.

6 Help Fijian children to receive you into their hearts and be friendly and kind to Indian children.

7 Help the new government to be fair to both Fijians and Indians.

Indians of Fiji

Sadly Fiji has not been a very happy country to live in recently. One hundred years ago people from India came to Fiji to work on the sugar plantations. Now there are roughly as many Indians as Fijians in the population of 770,000. The non-Indians are afraid that Fiji will be taken over by the Indians.

Fijians feel that the country belongs to them and were angry when the Fiji Labor Party, which tried to unite Indians and Fijians, won the election. The army got rid of the elected government and gave back power to the former Prime Minister.

The Indian people felt angry and afraid and many of them left Fiji.

Some Fijians behaved very badly indeed. The Indians in Fiji are Muslims, Hindus, or Sikhs. The Fijians say they are Christians, but some of them set fire to mosques and Hindu temples belonging to the Indians. Christian leaders spoke out strongly against this dreadful behavior. It made it very difficult for the Indians to believe that Jesus loved them.

There have now been many changes in the way the country is ruled, so that there will always be more Fijians elected to the government than Indians.

Some Christians have been able to make friends with Indian people and to invite their children to Sunday school. A few Hindu men and women have become Christians. Remember, when we meet people with different languages, ways of life, and religions from ours we must treat them with love and kindness.

FALASHAS

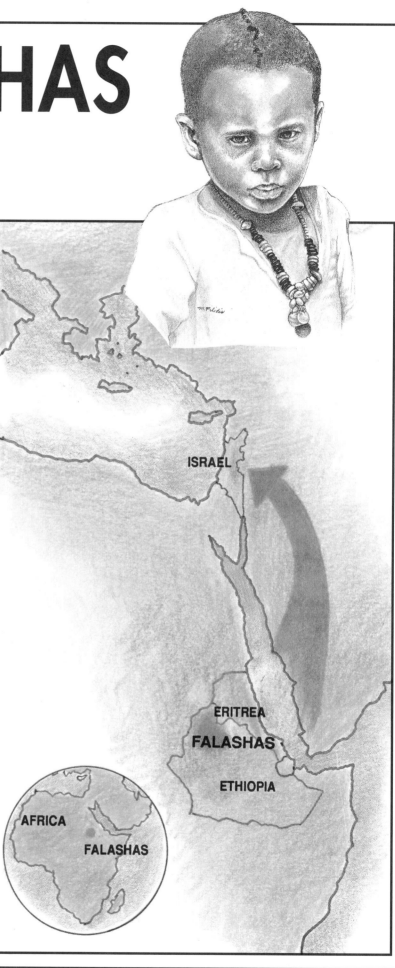

JEWS OF AFRICA

Did you know that there are black African Jews? Well, there are, called the Falashas. The word "falasha" means "stranger" or "someone without rights" in the Amharic language of Ethiopia, where they come from. They call themselves "the house of Israel" or "black Jews of Ethiopia." Even in Bible times there were probably Jews living in Ethiopia, so they shouldn't really be called strangers after more than two thousand years, should they?

There are no reliable records of their history, but many stories. Are they perhaps descendants of Menelek, the legendary son of King Solomon and the Queen of Sheba? No one knows, but in spite of persecution they continue to be faithful to the Jewish religion.

ISRAEL

ERITREA

FALASHAS

ETHIOPIA

AFRICA

FALASHAS

F for Falashas,
Africa's Jews;
They would all go to
Israel if they could choose.

Spies?

Missionaries gave the Falashas medical care and some became Christians. Later, Jews from Europe visited and then the Falashas wanted to go to Israel. Because of this, the Ethiopian government accused them of being spies; their villages were destroyed, their property taken, and some were tortured and killed.

"Operation Moses"

The Falashas' sufferings were increased by famine and civil war (see the section on Ethiopia – page 24). Thousands journeyed on foot to refugee camps in the neighboring country of Sudan, hoping eventually to reach Israel. They were contacted by the Israelis and an exciting rescue plan called "Operation Moses" began, arranged by the American, Israeli, and Sudanese governments. It was kept secret. If it had got into the newspapers it would have been stopped immediately as Sudan, a Muslim country, did not want to be seen helping Israel and the Jews.

Thirteen thousand of these Falashas were flown to Israel before the story leaked out. "Operation Moses" stopped abruptly, stranding many Falashas in Ethiopia and Sudan. Since then a new agreement allowed a Jewish agency to airlift the remaining seventeen thousand Falashas to Israel. Three thousand of these are Christians and the agency refused to take them. This divided families where there are both Jews and Christians. Israel's Chief Rabbi hopes that if the Falasha Christians are taken to Israel, they might become Jews again. So the government is considering whether or not to allow Christian Falashas into Israel.

Will Israel be a "promised land" for the Falashas? So far, life in Israel has not been easy for them. Their Jewish religious rules are stricter than those of most Jews in modern Israel; yet at the same time some Israelis won't accept them as true Jews. Israel's modern way of life frightens them. Gas, electricity, and flush toilets are completely new to them. Many have illnesses and have suffered from the loss of loved ones and attacks from bandits during the long trek to the refugee camps in Sudan.

You can pray for the Falashas

1 Dear Lord, show the Falashas that their journey to God does not end when they arrive in Israel, but when they put their trust in you.

2 Help the Falashas to settle down in Israel, which is so different from the Ethiopian villages they have left.

3 Help the Israeli government to be sympathetic to the Falasha Christians and allow them to join their people in Israel.

4 Give the Falasha Christians boldness to tell their families and friends about their faith in you.

5 The Falashas have suffered so much already; help Israeli Christians to share your love with them.

6 Help Falasha children as they go to school in Israel and have to adapt to a completely different way of life.

7 Please give them good friends who will not be unkind to them just because they are black.

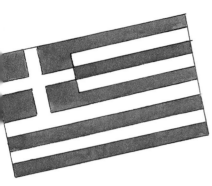

GREECE

WHERE THE FIRST OLYMPIC GAMES WERE HELD

No singing!

Dimitris liked the music and singing of the young people in the street. *What is it all about?* he wondered.

Suddenly a priest appeared and began arguing with them. A crowd quickly gathered, and when a woman tried to photograph what was going on, the priest snatched the camera out of her hand. Dimitris looked on with great interest and wondered what was going to happen next!

"Dimitris, what are you doing? Come along at once." The boy's grandmother grabbed his arm and pulled him away. "Those dreadful evangelicals arguing with a priest! Whatever will they do next?" she scolded.

"Oh no, grandmother. The priest started it," Dimitris explained. "Why did he do that? The music was lovely; they were singing about Jesus."

"Of course the priest was angry; they're heretics," grumbled his grandmother, pushing him in front of her across the road. "It's against the law for them to do such things; they aren't part of our Orthodox Church."

Like most Greek boys Dimitris, aged nine, had only been to church a few times. His grandmother bought him a candle, lit it, and made him bow down in front of a picture of a saint. He made the sign of the cross, kissed the picture, and left the candle beside it. These pictures, called icons, were all around the church. There were no

seats. He wondered how his old grandmother could stand for so long. "This is heaven," she whispered. "See the saints, Christ and the angels. We all meet together here."

The Olympics

The Olympic Games began in the eighth century B.C. in the Greek town of Olympia and continued until the fourth century A.D. as part of a religious festival. The modern games were first held in

Athens in 1896 and the Greeks would like the 1996 games to be held there too.

Modern Greece has beautiful beaches, ancient ruins, unspoiled islands and villages which haven't changed in centuries. Because of its beauty, more than nine million tourists visit Greece every year for wonderful vacations. But fewer than a hundred missionaries have gone to tell the Greeks about the love of Jesus.

Costas and the Morning Star

In Acts 16:9 we read how the apostle Paul was called in a vision to go and help take the good news about Jesus to Macedonia, which is part of modern Greece. Costas Macris, a Greek evangelist, is calling Christians today to come and help. He and his team act, sing, preach, and give out booklets on the streets. They also visit some of the many islands and coastal towns in their sailing boat, the Morning Star.

Costas and two other friends were sentenced to three and a half years in jail for giving a boy a New Testament. The three men went to the Appeal Court and after four days of trial they were found innocent.

G

stands for Greece, where Paul was so brave, Yet many don't know of the truths that he gave.

You can pray for Greece

1 Lord Jesus, please send more workers to serve you in Greece.

2 Give encouragement and boldness to those who know you as their own Savior.

3 Help Christians to work together in love to see Greek people reached with your truth.

4 Help young people to be brave and tell adults and children, even on the streets, about you.

5 May cassettes, books, and Christian newspapers help people to understand more about you.

6 May Orthodox priests listen to what the evangelicals have to say and come to know you personally.

7 Keep the Morning Star safe at sea, and help the crew to bring your Word to many people.

GYPSIES

NOMADS OF EUROPE AND THE WORLD

Where did the thirty-five million Gypsies in the world originally come from? No one really knows, but some say Egypt and others India. They are found in nearly every European country and in many other parts of the world too. Most speak one of the twenty or so Romany languages. Some people think they are dirty or thieves and some dislike and neglect them. As they are often nomads moving from place to place, some schools refuse to accept Gypsy children, so they cannot make friends with other children or learn to read.

Gypsies love children and teach them to be respectful to older people and not to talk to strangers. They have many rules about cleanliness which came long ago from the Indian Hindu religion (see page 116). They are very particular about their food. Muslim Rom Gypsies will not eat pork but like chicken; while Kaale Rom from Finland think chickens are dirty. Some Gypsies eat hedgehogs but others think them unclean. Gypsies like dancing and singing especially at weddings, where they may feast and dance for three days.

Thousands of "Gorgios" (non-Gypsies) in Britain and South Africa became Christians when a Gypsy, Rodney Smith, preached to them in 1901. He was asked, "Why don't you preach to Gypsies?" He replied, "The time has not yet come for the Gypsy people." But recently God has been working in the hearts of Gypsies in many parts of the world. In Britain alone more than five thousand Gypsies have become Christians since 1950.

Clara's discovery

Clara, a young woman of twenty, lived with her parents in their Gypsy caravan. As a child she had been to school on and off but never long enough to learn to read. She had heard about God's love for her but had never put her trust in Jesus.

One night she was very unhappy because she had been arguing with her parents. She knelt and prayed that God would help her to read the Bible so that she would know the right way to live. She was very disappointed that nothing seemed to happen.

The next morning she was helping her mother clean the caravan when she found an old Bible. Opening it at the Gospel of Matthew she was amazed to discover that she could read it! Excitedly she told her mother, who couldn't believe it until Clara read to her.

A few weeks later Clara understood fully what Jesus had done for her, and she put her trust in him. Ever since she has been telling people about God's special gift to her and, more importantly, about his gift of forgiveness and new life in Jesus.

Gypsies worldwide

Life is often difficult for Gypsies, but God's Holy Spirit is bringing many of them hope and peace. European Gypsies are sending money to help Gypsies in India and Madagascar, and going as missionaries to Gypsies in Argentina and the CIS (the old Soviet Union). France alone has sent Gypsy Christians to preach in twenty-four countries. Gypsy evangelist Tom Wilson said, "We Gypsies are a nation of evangelists: we can't help gossiping the gospel!"

You can pray for the Gypsies

1 Dear Lord, thank you that European Gypsies are going to tell other Gypsies throughout the world about your love and salvation.

2 Please call Christians to translate the Bible and make cassettes in the Romany languages and their many dialects.

3 Help Tom Wilson and other Gypsy evangelists in Britain to win more Gypsies for you.

4 Please send teachers to Gypsy children who move about and cannot go to school.

5 Send teachers to help French Gypsies learn to read the Bible.

6 Provide Bible training for British Gypsies who haven't been to school. Help them to be good teachers, evangelists, and pastors.

7 Work by your Holy Spirit among the Gypsies of Eastern Europe who have such an uncertain future.

HAITI

THE LAND FREED BY SLAVES

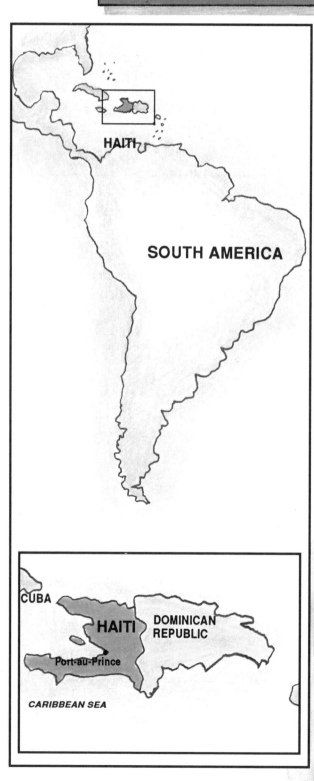

Haiti is half of an island called Hispaniola in the beautiful Caribbean Sea. (The other half is the Dominican Republic.) Nearly two hundred years ago Haiti's French rulers kidnapped people from West Africa and made them work as slaves in Haiti. One day they said, "Why should we be slaves? Let's fight for our freedom." After thirteen years of rebellion they managed to take control and rule the country themselves.

Sadly, Haiti has not been free since then, but has had one dictator after another, such as "Baby Doc" Duvalier. While he was in power it seems he stole eight hundred million dollars from his poor country.

Although riots, strikes, fear, and poverty are part of everyday life, love can still be found in Haiti. The love of Jesus is being preached by missionaries, Haitian ministers, and over the radio.

"Baby Doc."

Witchdoctor's son

At boarding school in Haiti, Gerard, a witch-doctor's son, listened to Christian programs on the radio his father had given him. His friend Louis was surprised. "Why do you listen to a missionary radio station? Aren't you going to be a witchdoctor one day?" he asked.

"Yes, but I like the Bible studies, and the music is really great," Gerard replied. At home he listened to the programs with his sister. His father heard them, and was furious. "Don't you ever listen to that station again! If you become a Christian, I'll drive you out of the house with a whip," he shouted.

Soon after, Gerard became very ill and none of the medicine, screaming, and drum-beating his father tried did any good. Rosselyn, Gerard's

sister, listened to the story of Elijah on the radio. "God answered Elijah by sending fire down on his sacrifice, even though it was wet with water," she told Gerard. "The men who worshiped other gods shouted and made a noise all day, just like we are doing, but got no answer at all. Why don't you pray to the Christians' God?"

"I don't know how to pray to him, or how to become a Christian."

"Why don't you write to the missionaries and ask them?" asked

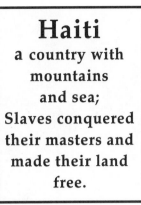

Haiti
a country with mountains and sea; Slaves conquered their masters and made their land free.

Rosselyn. "I'll get you some paper and a pen."

An answer came from the missionaries, but Gerard didn't quite understand it. Still feeling ill, he rode a bus

to the radio station. He had to walk part of the way and often had to sit down to rest by the road-side. At last he arrived and the missionary who had replied to him gave Gerard medicine and explained to him how to become a Christian. Gerard asked Jesus to forgive his sins and be his friend. He wanted to know Jesus so much he was no longer afraid of his father. Others, like Gerard, are finding out about Jesus through radio programs.

Voodoo

Most Haitians would say that they are Christians but few really know Jesus. Many practice voodoo in which evil spirits are worshiped, which is disobeying God's first commandment. Worship of spirits brings fear and sadness; evil spirits can take control of people and make them do strange, frightening, and sometimes cruel things.

You can pray for Haiti

1 Lord Jesus, please free the people of Haiti from the power of voodoo spirits.

2 Send Christians to tell of your love and care for those who are poor and ill-treated.

3 Give the country fair and just rulers who know what is best for the people.

4 Fill Christians with your joy and peace and help them to share them with others.

5 Use the radio pro-grams to explain how Jesus forgives us for all the things we have done wrong.

6 Fill the missionaries with your Holy Spirit and show them how to teach young people and children about you.

7 Send people to show your love to children who are hungry and afraid.

HERERO

CHILDREN OF THE OMUMBORUMBONGA TREE

Questioning the tree

The Herero people, who live in Namibia, southwest Africa, believed that at the beginning of time a man and a woman came out of the Omumborumbonga tree. It is a large, twisted, ancient-looking tree that grows in the dry bush country where the Herero graze their cattle.

The man was called "Mukuru," the first ancestor, and his wife was "Kamungundu." Even today when some Hereros pass the Omumborumbonga tree they will bow, put a bunch of grass into the branches, ask it questions, and then change their voices and pretend to answer themselves!

They believed a god "Karunga" is present everywhere and that people have souls that go to heaven after death. They wanted to be good in word and deed so they could approach "Karunga" clean and fresh as the rain. "Karunga," they believed, sent a flood to punish people for quarrelling. So when missionaries told them about God the Creator, Adam and Eve, the great flood of Noah, and Jesus, who is able to make people's lives clean and fresh, they found it easy to believe.

M. Filidis

HERERO
NAMIBIA
•WINDHOEK
SOUTH AFRICA
AFRICA

H for Herero with ladies serene; Their Victorian dresses are fit for a queen.

Holy fire

But there are other old beliefs which they have not given up. Some Herero people worship their dead relatives at a fire which they think is holy. They believe if the fire goes out the tribe will die out too. Onion skins must not be thrown away but be put on the holy fire, and people should not look at twins, blue skies, or their chief. These taboos and many others make the people afraid.

When a person becomes a true Christian and stops worshiping at the sacred fire, the elders often become angry. A young Herero couple, Alphons and Poppi, refused to worship at the fire on their wedding day. "We can't serve Jesus and Satan. We belong to Jesus alone," they said.

Perhaps they will be brave like Ananias Hiamuhona, a poor Herero shepherd who went to South Africa in 1945 to preach about Jesus. He is still working there, the first Herero missionary, full of Jesus' love and joy.

War and peace

In 1904 there was terrible fighting in Namibia. More than seventy thousand of the Herero people were killed and only twenty thousand were left alive. It has taken them many years to recover from that war, but now there are almost as many people as there were then. Most live in Hereroland, East Namibia, while some live near the capital, Windhoek. The women wear big head-dresses and ankle-length dresses with long sleeves. The dresses are like those worn by lady missionaries a hundred years ago.

The first missionaries translated the New Testament into the Herero language, but the whole Bible was not completed until 1988. Pray that as Hereros read the Old Testament they will understand that it is wrong to worship dead relatives. Most Hereros think they are Christians even when they still do this.

You can pray for the Herero

1 Dear Lord, please send teachers to Herero villages who will help both adults and children to want to know who you are.

2 Send missionaries to medical clinics in Hereroland so that they may help the sick people get better.

3 Help evangelists who speak in the schools to explain how much you love children and still care about them when they are poor, unhappy, or afraid.

4 Teach Herero students at Bible college so they can help others to trust you and obey the Bible.

5 Show the Herero people that only you can make their lives clean so that they can go to heaven.

6 Help the Herero people to see that worshiping the sacred fire and their dead relatives is wrong and harmful.

7 Thank you for Ananias who has told many people about you. Help other Herero people understand how wonderful it is to work for you too.

INDONESIA

THE LAND WHERE GOD WORKED MIRACLES

Many languages

Believe it or not, the country of Indonesia has 13,500 islands. To visit one each day would take almost thirty-seven years! The main islands are Bali, Irian Jaya, Java, Kalimatan, Sulawesi, Sumatra, and Timor. There are 180 million people in Indonesia, and more than six hundred languages are spoken, but in school everyone learns Indonesian, the national language. Although Indonesia has plenty of wealth from gas, oil, minerals and timber, many people are very poor.

War broke out in 1965 when Communists tried to take over the country by force. Petrus was then only eight years old, but still remembers how frightened he was. "It was very confused," he says, "On one side were the Communists, and on the other side the Muslims. The Muslims were so scared that they killed anyone they thought was a Communist. We longed for peace.

"Then everything changed. When the government defeated the Communists, they brought back an old law that said everyone had to choose a religion. My father didn't want to be a Muslim, because they had been so cruel to the Communists. Some people chose to be Hindu, others Buddhist, but we became Christians because we saw how kind and forgiving they were to other people."

In the next few years some amazing things happened as the good news about Jesus was preached. Sick people were healed and dead people were brought back to life. About two million people became Christians and were baptized. They did not all understand what it meant to be a Christian, but missionaries and evangelists were able to help them.

At present many Muslim leaders are unhappy because Christians are still free to preach and teach the Bible, and because the number of Christians keeps growing.

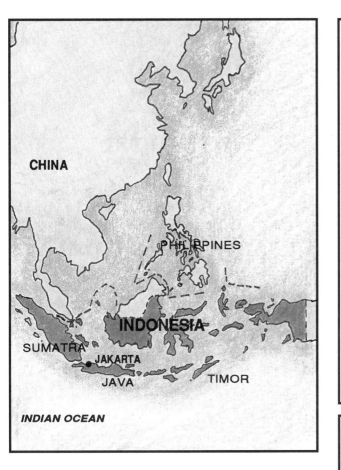

A sea goddess

Java is a beautiful island, with fertile soil, terraced rice fields, and volcanoes. Jakarta, the busy, crowded capital city of all Indonesia, is on this island. Three main people groups live on Java. These are the Sundanese and Madurese, who are nearly all Muslims, and the Javanese. A lot of Javanese have become Christians.

Before the people of Indonesia had to choose a religion, many were animists. Even now they keep some of their old ways. Some worship the "goddess of the southern seas" in ceremonies that take place in the sea. Sometimes people drown during the ceremony, and it is believed the sea goddess has taken them. Other people worship spirits and practice harmful magic. Even

important government officials throw money and even live animals into active volcanoes as sacrifices.

Parts of Indonesia are so difficult to reach that the people who live there have never heard God's Word. Who will be the very first Christians to go and live in these islands, to teach the truth about Jesus and bring people to know and love him?

I for Indonesia, where God moved in power By sending revival in her darkest hour.

The prophet Isa

Although more Muslims have become Christians in Indonesia than anywhere else in the world, it is not easy for them. Enjang was only six when he started to study the Koran. "I get scared when I read the Koran," he told his uncle. "I'm afraid of hell." Enjang's uncle said, "In the Koran you can read about the prophet Isa, Mary's son. That could help you." Enjang read about Isa and became less troubled.

Soon he realized that Isa is the Muslim name for Jesus. "I began to love him so much that I became a Christian. I started to tell other Muslim children about Jesus. But their parents were furious. My brother beat me up and threw me out of our village. I was sad about this, but I know that Jesus loves us so much that I must go on telling people about him."

You can pray for Indonesia

1 Lord Jesus, please help people like Enjang who suffer when they become Christians.

2 Help Christians in Indonesia to show your love to those of other religions. Help people give up spirit worship.

3 Help those writing and sending out correspondence courses to make people think about Jesus.

4 Send people with your message to every inhabited island in Indonesia.

5 Use Bible colleges to train evangelists, pastors, and missionaries, and fill them with your Holy Spirit.

6 Send people to tell the Sundanese and Madurese Muslims of Java of the peace and joy that they can find in you.

7 Help many of the children of Indonesia to follow and trust you.

IRULA

SNAKE CATCHERS OF SOUTHERN INDIA

I for the Irula who catch snakes alive,
Then milk out their venom and let them survive.

Mara, a ten-year-old Irula boy, couldn't sleep. He could hear the gentle breathing of his parents, brother, and two sisters, who were sleeping on the floor beside him. As soon as it was light he was going with his father to catch poisonous snakes. He felt excited – and scared.

He thought about the captured snakes that were kept in mud pots in the hut next to his home. Sometimes the snakes laid eggs in these pots, and Mara's father would carefully hatch them out before releasing the wriggling babies into the forest.

Mara was very happy to set off next day with his father, who was playing an Irula flute through his nose as he walked along. The first snake they caught was a cobra.

Mara's father showed him some marks on the scales of its belly.

"This one has already been 'milked' three times this year," he explained. "We make these marks to show we mustn't milk it again till next year or it will get exhausted and die." Soon the basket Mara carried was heavy with snakes and his arms ached, but he didn't complain in case his father wouldn't take him again.

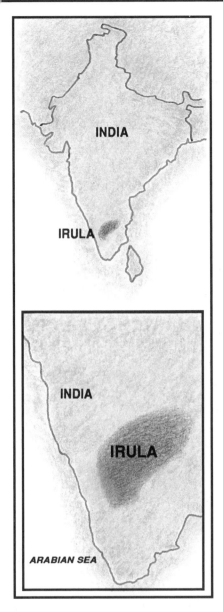

A cure for snake bites

For many years the Irula people caught snakes for their skins. In just one year ten million were sold overseas to make snakeskin shoes, bags, and purses. This is now illegal because the Indian government wants wildlife, including snakes, to be preserved.

Instead, as about twenty thousand Indians are bitten by poisonous snakes every year, the Irula now collect and sell snake venom to be used as an antidote to snake bites, and in medicines to cure certain kinds of serious illness.

The snake is pinned to the ground with a stick and its head held between the thumb and first finger. Its jutting fangs are pressed against a sheet of rubber stretched over a glass jar. The snake bites the rubber sheet and the deadly venom trickles into the jar.

devils and tigers. Their language is a mixture of three Indian languages and sounds like a sweetly hummed tune. Some Indian missionaries are translating the Bible into their language, giving medical help, supplying food for the poor, and teaching about Jesus. They are also teaching some Irulas to read.

At the moment there are very few Irula Christians and the children are often very afraid of the devils, tigers, gods, and goddesses they worship. Not many know about the true God who sent Jesus to set them free from fear.

A frightened people

The one hundred thousand Irula are shy and poor, owning only a few water buffalo, cattle, and sheep. They live in the hills of southern India, where they grow fruit, vegetables, and grain. They sell wild honey, drink coffee flavored with salt, and collect jungle fruits and roots.

The Irula have curly hair, broad noses, dark features, and are very small. Few children go to the schools, which are far from their forest homes. Schooling must be paid for and besides, the children are needed to help at home.

Although they live among Hindus, the Irula are animists and worship, among other things,

You can pray for the Irula

1 Dear Lord, please help Indian missionaries to learn the Irula language and to translate the Bible into it.

2 Help Irula people to want to learn to read, so that they can find out for themselves how much you love them.

3 Help the Irula understand that worshiping spirits will only bring them fear but Jesus will give them peace and joy.

4 Send Indian missionaries to teach Irula children that you care for them and want to remove their fear.

5 Thank you for the Indian missionaries who are living in Irula villages. Help them to explain clearly the good news about Jesus.

6 Help the Masthri family, the first Irula Christians, to be so much like Jesus that their friends would like to become Christians too.

7 Send your Holy Spirit so that Irula people may understand the Bible and become happy, loving Christians.

JAPAN

LAND OF THE RISING SUN

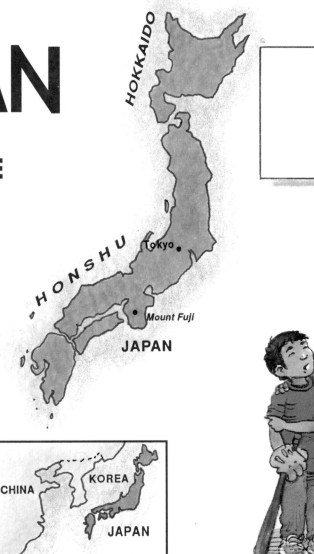

The flag of Japan shows the rising sun, symbol of the sun goddess. The Japanese are taught that their Emperor Akihito descended from her. He was made emperor in a special ceremony when he was said to hold a secret meeting with the sun goddess and so himself became a god who must be worshiped.

Emperor worship is called Shintoism, but its followers also worship the sun, Mount Fuji (a mountain in Japan), the fox god, the snake god, spirits of water and fire, and many other things. Shintoism is part of Japanese culture and school children visit Shinto temples as part of their education.

If Shintoism becomes really strong, preaching about Jesus could be stopped. This has happened twice before. Shintoists can't understand why Christians refuse to worship at Shinto temples, since worshiping more than one god doesn't matter to them. So the Japanese feel they would be turning against their family and their culture if they only worshiped Jesus.

Mount Fuji.

Too many lessons!

Toshio was angry. "I don't want to take lessons after school," he grumbled to his mother. "I want to join the baseball club. Why must I work all day and night?"

"Stop shouting, Toshio! Your father will hear you. I know you want to join the baseball club, but that won't get you into university or get you a good job."

"I don't care about university or a good job. They haven't made Daddy happy. He can't do the things he likes — he's always working, working, working. I want to have fun with my friends."

"Toshio, you are naughty! You won't pass your exams, then what will the neighbors think of me?" Toshio's mother sighed. Toshio picked up his baseball glove and bat and ran from the house. He felt like crying. His mother was always worrying about what the neighbors might think. "They're more important to her than I am," he thought bitterly.

J

for Japan, where courtesy reigns; With beautiful ladies – and very full trains!

Robot workers

Not all Japanese children feel like Toshio. Although they go to school on Saturday mornings and have five or six hours of home-work every day, some still want extra lessons to make sure they pass their exams! Many are willing to give up sports, watch-ing television, and play-ing with their friends to get good marks.

Toshio has a computer and many toys and books, and his parents and elder brothers all have cars. Japan makes more cars and electronic toys and products than any other country. For example, in Japan there are thousands of robots – making goods, cleaning sewers, scaring birds away from crops, washing windows, and picking oranges.

The family shrine

The Japanese often live to be very old. Toshio has grandparents and great-grandparents. His mother cares for his great-grand-mother, bathing her and tenderly brushing her snowy white hair. She is very religious and worships at the family shrine each day, scolding Toshio's mother for not doing so.

You can pray for Japan

1 Lord Jesus, please help Japanese Christians to be brave enough to worship you and not bow down to idols.

2 Help missionaries to know how best to tell Japanese people the truth about Jesus.

3 Please help Emperor Akihito to become a Christian and tell the people he is not a god.

4 Help Japanese people not to be afraid of being different from others and dare to follow you.

5 Please stop the government from making laws that force people to worship at Shinto shrines.

6 Please help children to love you so much that although they have lots of homework, they will make time to pray to you and learn more about you.

7 Thank you that your Word has been preached in Japan for many years. Help people to stop following false gods, so that you alone may be worshiped there.

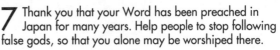

JOLAS

WHO PRAY TO THE SPIRITS IN POEMS

Ampa's week-old baby brother wriggled as his head was shaved by a Jola elder. The old man chewed betel nut as he worked and then spat some red-stained saliva onto the baby's head. "This will protect the baby's heart," he said. Then the old man blew and prayed into the baby's tiny ears. A few feet away a chicken was being sacrificed to please the spirits so that they would look after the baby.

Ampa was very ill when he was ten and his father asked the priest to pray for him. The priest prayed in a poem he made up on the spot. He told the spirit that Ampa was ill and his father had brought palm wine and a chicken as a gift. In his poem he asked one spirit to tell another spirit, to tell another spirit, and so on, until eventually a spirit told the creator god. Sadly Ampa's family did not know the true Creator God – though some of the sixty-five thousand Jola people who live in Gambia, West Africa, are beginning to hear about him.

Elizabeth's friends

Elizabeth, a thirteen-year-old Jola girl, lived with her mother, aunt, and brothers in a single room in Banjul, Gambia's capital. Every day she went with other young people to the home of the missionaries, Anne and Shirley, across the street. Elizabeth, shy and quiet, wanted someone to take an interest in her. The missionaries asked her mother if she might sleep and study in their home. Elizabeth was so happy when her mother agreed.

Elizabeth studied hard and enjoyed singing and praying, sewing classes and Bible studies in Anne and Shirley's home. Though living with the missionaries, Elizabeth was still very much part of her own family. Every lunch time she raced home to cook for them, and each evening she fried fish cakes for her mother to sell.

One day Elizabeth asked Jesus to forgive her sins and to come into her life. Things then became very different at home and at school. Instead of being shy she became brave enough to tell others about Jesus, and she refused to do wrong things.

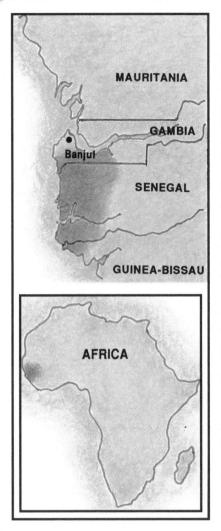

Elizabeth grows up

Elizabeth then went to typing school, and after a while the school paid for her to qualify as a teacher herself. She was very grateful for all God had done for her because it is extremely hard to get jobs in Banjul. After she started teaching, Elizabeth was very happy buying treats for her mother and brothers, which she hadn't been able to do before.

In Gambia, thousands of children need opportunities like those Elizabeth has had. Knowing this, Elizabeth gave up her job in Banjul and moved to a small town, Sibanor, to work in a Christian Youth Center where she could help other children learn as she had done. Telling children how Jesus has changed her life makes her happier than ever.

Not many Jolas have left their spirit worship and put their trust in Jesus. The Evangelical Church is growing, however, and in Gambia six congregations are meeting. There is one Jola pastor and one Christian worker – guess who? Yes, that's right: Elizabeth!

J for the Jola whose babies, it's said, Are protected from harm by a spit on the head!

You can pray for the Jolas

1 Dear Lord, please help Elizabeth as she teaches the Bible to school children and runs a girls' sewing class.

2 Help the children at the Youth Center to understand all that you have done for them and to enjoy the fun and games they have together.

3 Show Elizabeth's brother, Momodou, that he needs to put his trust in you.

4 Help Jola young men to be strong Christians and to tell others about your love and power.

5 Help Christian mothers to show your love in their homes, so that their husbands and children may come to know you too.

6 Help many Jola people to believe in Jesus and set them free from evil spirits.

7 Help Jola Christians to make up beautiful poems and songs to worship you.

SOUTH KOREA

LAND OF THE MORNING CALM

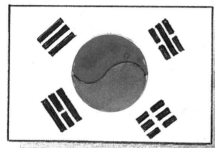

A divided land

The Korean flag shows the Chinese yin-yang symbol. The lines represent the four seasons, the points of the compass, and the earth, heaven, sun, and moon.

Called the "Land of the Morning Calm," Korea is a beautiful country. Its rivers, mountains, forests, colorful flowers, plants, and birds have inspired Korean poets, painters, and potters. Koreans love music and dancing and are gifted singers.

Unfortunately Korea has not had true peace for fifty years. After the Second World War the country was split into two, North Korea and South Korea. But the North attacked the South. The North became a Communist country, while the South had a government which was much more open to the rest of the world.

SOUTH KOREA

CHINA

NORTH KOREA

● Seoul

SOUTH KOREA

Returning home

Byung Kook Yoo, his wife Bo In, and their daughters Jean, Lam, and baby Yevon were very excited. They were returning to South Korea from Gambia, West Africa (see the Jolas, page 46) where they had been missionaries for five years. Jean and Lam didn't remember much about Korea and wondered how they would find life there.

"Remember to take off your shoes whenever you go into a house," Bo In told them.

"What will we eat, Mommy?" Lam asked. "I hope I can eat nicely with chopsticks."

"Don't worry, Lam, you'll soon get used to them. We'll use a spoon for rice and fish as we

K

for Korea, where the Christians are many; That's in the South – in the North, hardly any.

did in Gambia. You'll like kimchi." Kimchi, a kind of pickle, is made by mixing vegetables with spices and other strongly flavored foods.

Byung Kook looked proudly at his daughters. Most Korean men badly want sons, but he wouldn't change his lovely girls for any boy. At school in Gambia they told Muslim friends

about Jesus and even held Bible studies with some of the children. He wondered how they would get on at school in Korea. It is hard in a class of sixty children to get individual attention, and they had forgotten some Korean words.

Korean children usually go to schools like ours and learn similar subjects. They have to practice writing their difficult language, and have lots of homework. They don't have much time to watch television! In Korea only educated people are honored and respected, so schoolwork is especially important.

On Sunday mornings in the capital city, Seoul, thousands of people go along to church. There are nearly five thousand churches in the city. Although Buddhism*

was the ancient religion of Korea, today in South Korea there are as many Christians as Buddhists. The largest Christian meeting ever held in the world was in Korea, attended by more than two and a half million people. About 1,900 missionaries like Byung Kook and Bo In have gone to more than eighty-seven different countries, and every year Koreans print Bibles in hundreds of different languages to send around the world.

Every day in South Korea six new churches are opened. When we realize what God has done in the South, we should pray for North Korea too. Christianity is still forbidden there, and very few people know about the love of Jesus.

* See page 115.

* See page 115.

You can pray for Korea

1 Lord Jesus, thank you for the many true Christians in Korea who pray to you every day and love to worship you.

2 Help Bible students to love you and your Word with all their hearts.

3 Thank you for the many Christian groups like Campus Crusade and Navigators who work with young people.

4 Help missionaries' children like Jean and Lam to feel that they belong in Korea when they go home on vacation.

5 May missionaries like Byung Kook and Bo In help other Korean people to be missionaries too.

6 Send Korean Christians who are full of your Holy Spirit to make Jesus known all over Asia.

7 May the people of North Korea who haven't been allowed to hear about you or worship you, find out that you love them.

KURDS

A PEOPLE WITHOUT A HOME

Shakkak snuggled closer to Tim on the rug in his tent. He lives in an isolated Kurdish village in the land of Turkey. Shakkak liked Tim's kind smiling face but couldn't understand what Tim was saying, because he was deaf. Other village boys were out guarding the sheep, but because of his deafness Shakkak had to stay behind in the tent.

Tim is a Christian from Europe who wants to tell the Kurdish people about Jesus. As he walked towards Shakkak's village earlier that day he had prayed that God would do something special to make that possible.

An important envelope

When Tim left the village a few days later, he carried with him a crumpled envelope that would answer his prayer. That envelope

Kurds live in Turkey, Iran, and Iraq; A land of their own is what they most lack.

contained a prescription for a hearing aid for Shakkak. Hearing aids could only be bought in Istanbul, Turkey's biggest city, six hundred miles from Shakkak's home – and they cost more than his family could afford. Tim didn't have the money either, but he did have faith in God.

Several months later Tim returned to the village. God had provided money for the hearing aid and Tim was fingering it in his pocket. As it was placed in Shakkak's ear he was able to hear for the first time in his life! He was radiant, his face beaming with joy. Now Tim and his missionary friends are always welcome in Shakkak's village, and that gives them a great chance to share their faith in Jesus. God had answered Tim's prayer through Shakkak's deafness.

Ill-treated

The twenty-five million Kurdish people live mainly in the countries of Turkey, Iran, Iraq, and Syria. Today they are suffering terribly and do not feel completely safe or happy anywhere. They are persecuted by the governments of these countries because of their long and often violent struggle for "Kurdistan," a land of their own. The countries where they live are afraid that if they succeed, other people groups may want their own land too.

In Iran and Syria the Kurds have been treated cruelly by different governments. In Iraq they have been bombed and attacked with poison gas. Thousands died from lack of food and exposure to the cold while escaping to Turkey and Iran. Twelve million Kurds live in Turkey, where they are also unwanted, often ill-treated and were not allowed books or leaflets in their own language until 1991.

The Kurds are Muslims, but it has been mostly other Muslim people who have mistreated them. For many years Christians have wanted to take the message of Jesus' love to them, but the areas where they live have been difficult to reach. Since Christians have been allowed to give food and medicine to those in trouble the Kurds have been eager to hear stories about Jesus.

Some Kurds in Turkey have become Christians while studying the Bible, and others in Britain and Germany are hearing the good news about Jesus and putting their trust in him. These Kurds in the West are usually refugees or low-paid workers, but at least life is safer for them and their families than it used to be.

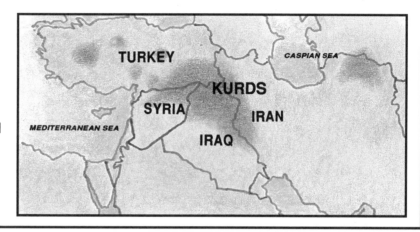

You can pray for the Kurds

1 Lord Jesus, please help Kurdish refugees from Iraq to be treated kindly in Turkey and Iran.

2 Make it possible for Christian cassettes and videos in Kurdish to be given out in Turkey and the other lands where Kurds live.

3 Show Christians how to get Christian literature to the Kurds in Iran and Syria.

4 Help those translating the New Testament into the three Kurdish languages to finish their work quickly.

5 Help refugees to be able to return to their own homes in peace.

6 Thank you that Christians in Britain, Germany, and other European countries are showing your love to Kurdish refugees.

7 Help Kurds all over the world to listen to your Word, and set them free from the power of Islam.

LESOTHO

THE SWITZERLAND OF AFRICA

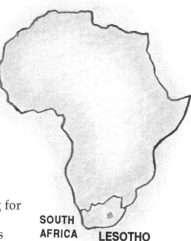

SOUTH
AFRICA   LESOTHO

Lesotho has spectacular mountains with flowing streams and rushing rivers, which is why some people call it "the Switzerland of Africa." Many of its villages can only be reached on horseback.

As sheep's wool and mohair (made from goat's hair) are the main exports of Lesotho, thousands of animals are herded by about sixty thousand shepherd boys. In summer rain and winter frost these lonely boys have little shelter, but they can enjoy beautiful scenery and fresh clean air. Sometimes they are away from their home villages for months on end.

The shepherd boys must look after their animals carefully, as they are very valuable. They will be in trouble if any sheep are injured or damage crops because the boys haven't done their job properly. Until a younger brother is old enough to take over for him, the shepherd boy cannot go to school, so girls are usually better educated than boys. The summer is a happy time for them, playing on the mountains and caring for their sheep as King David did many years ago in Judea.

Lesotho is a small country completely surrounded by South Africa. Its one and a half million people are called the Basotho, and their language Sotho. The people wear brightly-colored blankets and cone-shaped hats of woven grass, with babies being carried fastened to their mothers' or sisters' backs.

Because there are so few jobs to be found in Lesotho itself many men have to go to South Africa to work in the gold mines. They must miss their families very much.

Horseback teachers
Although most Basothos are members of the Roman Catholic or

L

for Lesotho,
where shepherd
boys work hard;
In winter and
summer they're
always on guard.

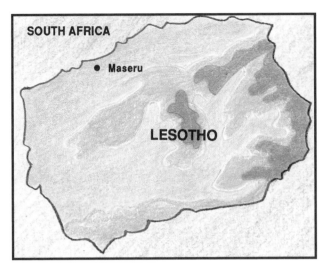

SOUTH AFRICA

● Maseru

LESOTHO

Fellowship (MAF) has built forty runways so that their planes can land nearby, to carry supplies to remote areas or take patients to the hospital. Mokeane, a little Basotho boy, broke his arm and the MAF pilot flew him to the capital, Maseru, where he had his arm put in a cast. The flight took only twenty-five minutes, but it would have taken more than nine hours for Mokeane's parents to take him by road.

Duncan and Dilys Threshie work with Scripture Union in Lesotho. They train teachers to run Christian groups in schools, teaching Scripture Union workers and producing Bible reading notes in the Sotho language. In vacation times there is great excitement as Duncan and Dilys hold Bible camps for the children.

You can pray for Lesotho

1 Lord Jesus, please keep the MAF pilots safe as they bring medical care and supplies to the villages and tell people of your love.

2 Use the "Jesus" film and other films to teach the people of Lesotho to know you.

3 Send "missionary cowboys" on horseback to the mountain villages to do medical work and visit the lonely shepherd boys.

4 Help those who receive Bible lessons through the mail to come to know you.

5 Be with the men who are away from home in the South African mines, and watch over their families, and teach them your love and truth.

6 Help Duncan and Dilys to teach men and women to become leaders in the Lesotho church and to love, obey, and worship you.

7 Be with the shepherd boys working alone on the mountains, and keep them safe as you did David in the Bible.

Lesotho Evangelical Church, few understand that Jesus died so they could be forgiven. Missionaries are training church leaders and sending them lessons through the mail. Once a month they meet for extra teaching and have to travel on horseback, by bus, or on foot to get to a training center.

Missionaries are needed who can ride horses and visit the distant villages, to tell the good news of Jesus and show

films such as the "Jesus" film. Thousands of people have watched this film of Jesus' life and teaching, miracles and death on the cross, and have asked him to come into their lives. Several churches have been started in remote villages through this film.

Many of the villages are far from roads, so the Mission Aviation

LOBI

WHO FILE THEIR TEETH TO POINTS

Why the scars?

About 250,000 Lobis live in the country of Burkina Faso in West Africa, and sixty-two thousand in neighboring Côte d'Ivoire. Years ago Lobi women had their faces scarred to make them look so ugly that slave traders wouldn't capture them. Holes were pierced in both lips, into which round pieces of wood were inserted. A few women like this can still be seen today.

Children who vanish

Sie watched the long line of people hurrying down the road – children, some not much bigger than himself; women carrying cooking pots and sacks of food on their heads; men cracking whips so that everyone moved quickly. He shivered as he heard the cries of the children, cries heard only once every seven years at the time of the *joro!* He was afraid, for he knew his turn would come!

The *joro* is the initiation ceremony of the Lobi people. Children of seven and older are taken from their parents into the bush for two to three months by

their tribal leaders. After many frightening tests of bravery, each child is presented to a large idol, the *joro*, the evil spirit who controls the initiation. The children's teeth are filed to points as a sign that they are true Lobis. Some children never return, and their families are not allowed to ask what has happened to them. It is enough to know that the *joro* spirit took them.

Although it is forbidden for anyone who has been initiated to talk about it to those who haven't, Sie knew enough to be very afraid. His family all had pointed teeth, but as he heard the eerie cries fading into the distance, he asked himself, "Must I go to that *joro* spirit too? Isn't there another way to become a true Lobi?"

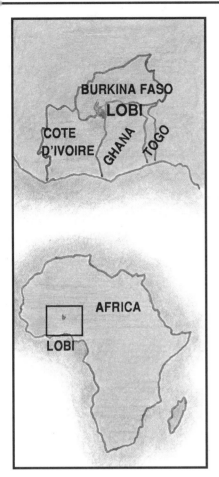

L stands for Lobi, fierce people and strong; Their worship of *joro* has made them do wrong.

Slaves no more

Their windowless homes are very big and built of mud, and the inner rooms are dark. Life-size idols made of clay are placed inside and outside the houses. From May to September most Lobis work in their fields to produce millet, corn, peanuts, and yams from the infertile soil. Only one adult out of every ten can read.

Few Lobis are real Christians, but more are coming to know Jesus. There are thirty churches, and fifty-eight trained Lobi Christian workers. Nako, the main center where initiation ceremonies take place, now has a church. The new Lobi translation of the New Testament was published in 1985.

Perhaps Sie will not have to go to the *joro* to become a true Lobi. Each time the initiation ceremonies are held, Christians pray for the spirits to lose their grip on the people and there are signs that this is happening. Lobi Christians are also telling other animistic and Muslim peoples of Burkina Faso about Jesus. May the slaves of the *joro*, who takes life, become the children of God.

You can pray for the Lobi

1 Dear Lord, please send workers to Lobi young people to help them to have faith in you, and to be free from fear.

2 Continue to free the Lobi people from the evil power of the *joro*.

3 Please help Lobi men and women in training at Bible college so that they can bring many others closer to Jesus.

4 Make your church in Nako so strong that the initiation ceremonies will lose their power and come to an end.

5 Help Christians learning to read to understand the New Testament in their own language.

6 Send Christians who love children to hold camps and meetings for them which they will enjoy.

7 May many Lobi Christians want to be missionaries to other tribes who live near them.

MONGOLIA

THE LAND WITH MORE HORSES THAN PEOPLE

The country of Mongolia is sandwiched between Russia and China, and is a land of windswept plains, mountains, forests, and deserts. For sixty-five years Mongolia was closed to the outside world by its Communist government, so when I met Udbal, a Mongolian student, I asked her lots of questions about this mysterious country.

Udbal grew up in Ulaan Baatar, which is Mongolia's capital and the only large city in the country. "Some people live in apartments in the city, but many prefer tents called *gers*," she said. "So houses and *gers* are all mixed together. The *gers* have electricity, so we can have TV and radio, but water has to be fetched from outside. Both my parents work, so my brothers, sisters, and I fetch water, chop wood, shop, cook, and clean."

"Do children have time to play with all that work to do?" I asked.

"Oh yes! In July we have a big sports festival with wrestling, archery, and horseracing. Almost everyone in Mongolia can ride and children aged five to eleven ride in exciting thirty-mile races."

"Is it true that you drink horses' milk?" I asked.

Udbal giggled.

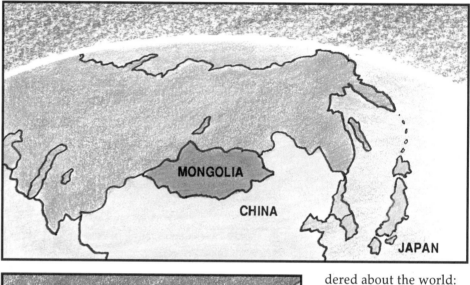

"Mares' milk, yes. It's fizzy after a few days and very refreshing. We make cheese from goat's and sheep's milk. Many people keep animals, even in the towns, where it is against the law.

Religion banned

Before the Communist government banned religion, Mongolia was strongly Buddhist. Families sent their eldest sons to be Buddhist monks. Buddhism was mixed with spirit worship and had an evil influence on the country.

I asked Udbal about Buddhism. "It was never mentioned at school, and at home my father is an atheist and doesn't believe in God. The Communists only allowed one Buddhist monastery to stay open. When I was little, I won-dered about the world: Who made it? Where do people come from? How can there be no God, as the Communists say? Most children puzzle about these things, but if we ask questions, we are told to be quiet."

For centuries no one was allowed to preach about Jesus in Mongolia. But in 1990 a miracle happened; the Communist government lost power and people were given the freedom to become Christians. Already there are three churches. Many young people have become interested in Christianity after seeing a film about the life of Jesus.

The New Testament has been translated into Mongolian and printed in a Russian script. It is also being printed in a special script used over the border in Inner Mongolia, which is part of China. Pray that Mongolians living in China may soon hear about Jesus too.

A special book

"How did you come to believe in Jesus?" I asked.

"It is wonderful. When I was a student, a man from overseas asked me to help translate the Bible. I thought it was a children's book because of the exciting stories. Gradually I saw it was a special book about God and his Son, Jesus. I believed in him, and began to trust him," answered Udbal.

Modern and traditional buildings of Mongolia, including a *ger* (*front left*).

You can pray for Mongolia

1 Lord Jesus, please stop Mongolians from going back to Buddhism now that they have more freedom to worship as they wish.

2 Help Mongolian boys and girls to wonder who made them and who created the world, so they may seek you and find you for themselves.

3 Send Christians to Mongolia to tell the people about your love and forgiveness.

4 Use the Mongolian New Testament to help many to trust in you. Help Christians to write and to translate Christian books into Mongolian.

5 Help Udbal and the other Mongolian Christians to be so joyful that their friends will want to know you.

6 Help the Mongolian Christian who is planning radio programs. May many people listen and to turn to you.

7 Thank you that schools and colleges are receiving Christian magazines in easy English. Use the stories to help many trust in Jesus.

MINANGKABAU

THE PEOPLE OF THE WATER BUFFALO

This is a legend about the seven million Minangkabau people who live on the island of Sumatra in Indonesia (see page 40). About six hundred years ago the king of the nearby island of Java wanted to rule Sumatra, so he sent the Minangkabau a message that he was about to take over their land. The Minangkabau were not strong enough to defend themselves, so they challenged the king of Java to a different type of contest.

"Let us both select a water buffalo," they suggested. "Let them fight each other. If your buffalo wins we will serve you, but if our buffalo wins you must never again attempt to conquer us." To this the king agreed.

So the king of Java sent all over Indonesia until he found the biggest, fiercest water buffalo possible. When the Minangkabau saw it, their hearts trembled. *We can never find a buffalo to beat this one*, they thought.

Suddenly they had an idea. They found a little buffalo calf and for three days kept him away from his mother. The poor little thing was desperate for his mother's milk. They covered his tiny horns with razor-sharp pieces of iron and sent him out to meet the giant buffalo. How the Javanese laughed! They thought they were certain to win.

All the little calf could think of was milk. He rushed towards the giant buffalo thinking it was his mother. Eagerly he thrust his little mouth under the buffalo looking for a drink. His sharp iron horns tore into the big buffalo's belly. Roaring in pain, the buffalo charged off with the calf in hot pursuit. Very soon the giant buffalo fell dead to the ground. "Minangkabau! Minangkabau!" the people shouted. "Our buffalo wins! Our buffalo is victorious!" The little calf had flowers hung around his neck, the pieces of iron were removed from his horns, and he was led back to his mother.

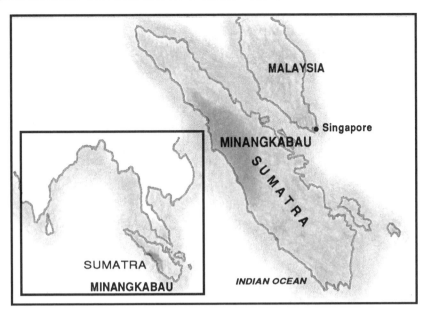

You can pray for the Minangkabau

1 Dear Lord, please use the healing and care of the Christian hospital to show Minangkabau people how much you love them.

2 Help people to want to read the Minangkabau New Testament and send your Holy Spirit to help them understand it.

3 Give courage and power to the few Minangkabau Christians to speak about you in their villages.

4 Teach Minangkabau men training to be pastors how to tell their own people that you are the Son of God.

5 Help missionaries and Minangkabau Christians to write songs and hymns they will enjoy singing.

6 Send Christians to teach the children about you.

7 Help Christians to make friends with Minangkabau businessmen in the towns and to share your love with them.

Can you think of true stories in the Bible like this where the weak triumphed over the strong? The story in 1 Samuel 17 is one of the best-known.

To be Minangkabau is to be Muslim, and they have opened the first Islamic college in Indonesia. So how can these people come to follow Jesus? The government has allowed churches to open and there are a few Christian Minangkabau. Pastors are being trained and the Minangkabau church is growing. The New Testament has been translated and some Christian books have been written in the Minangkabau language and there is a hospital run by Christians. Many people are praying for them because they are one of the three largest people groups in the world with very few Christians.

Women who farm

The Minangkabau are an unusual people, because it is the women rather than the men who own the land. Men often leave the villages to find work in the towns, only returning home to help at harvest time. Women prepare the soil, plant seedlings, and remove weeds. Buffalo are kept for plowing and for their milk, from which thin yogurt is made. Minangkabau people eat rice with vegetables seasoned with very hot chilies.

NEW ZEALAND

AOTEAROA – LAND OF THE LONG WHITE CLOUD

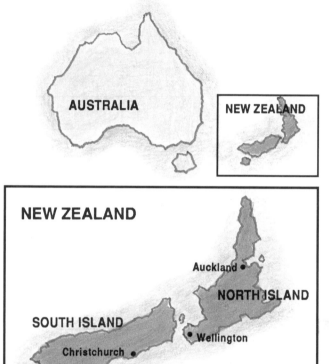

New Zealand has two main islands, simply called North Island and South Island. There are two main people groups, those who originally came from Britain and the more local Maori people. The Maoris call New Zealand the "land of the long white cloud" because the climate is often wet, windy, and cool. This is ideal for sheep farming. The three and a half million people keep more than seventy-three million sheep: that's over twenty sheep to every person!

New Zealand is a beautiful volcanic land with rolling hills, steep mountains, giant trees, and hot pools and springs. The people love sports and are known all over the world for their skill in rugby and cricket.

A kiwi.

For a joke, New Zealanders are often called Kiwis. Kiwis are birds which are found only in New Zealand. They look like a hen without a tail and have hardly any wings.

The Maoris originally came from the Pacific islands of Polynesia. They arrived many centuries ago in sixty-foot-long canoes, each carved from a single log. They built beautiful meeting places where tribes still gather. Maori children learn their history in action songs.

AUSTRALIA

NEW ZEALAND

NEW ZEALAND

Auckland

NORTH ISLAND

SOUTH ISLAND

Wellington

Christchurch

one in nine people reads the Bible regularly. The government has actually asked Indonesia (see page 40) to send Muslims to spread Islam in New Zealand and to provide money for the study of their religion. Albanian refugees (see page 8) introduced Islam into New Zealand in 1950. There are now eight mosques and Islamic centers in Auckland, the biggest city, Wellington, the capital, and Christchurch on the South Island.

N for New Zealand, whose mountains are steep; The land of the kiwi and millions of sheep.

They also learn how to cook food in leaves buried in the ground between hot stones. Seaweed, sweet potatoes, cabbages, beef, lamb, and pork taste delicious cooked in this way.

Maori children used to be punished for speaking their own language instead of English in school, until their leaders demanded their rights. "We've been here more than one thousand years, so why shouldn't we speak our own language?" they said.

Maori customs

Some Maoris have become strong Christians, but few are leaders as there isn't a Maori Bible school yet. Old customs are being revived by Maori artists, painters, craftsmen, and film producers and this could make Maoris become more interested in traditional myths and gods than they are in Christianity.

Few New Zealanders of either group believe that Jesus is the only way to God. Many say they are Christians but only

You can pray for New Zealand

1 Lord Jesus, please help Christians in New Zealand to speak eagerly about their faith in you to their friends and families.

2 Help Christians to talk to Muslims about you in a loving, caring way.

3 Help churches to do missionary work in New Zealand and to send missionaries to other lands.

4 Help Christians to give money for a Maori Bible school and help Maori preachers to show their people that they can become Christians too.

5 Send teachers who love children to hold Christian camps, clubs, and activities to help them follow you.

6 Help Albanians living in New Zealand to put their trust in you.

7 Help Christians of all races in New Zealand to love and care for each other and to serve you together.

NAVAJOS

SAND PAINTERS OF THE AMERICAN WEST

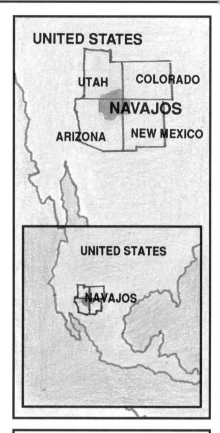

Navajos are the largest group of Indians in the USA and live in the western states of Arizona, New Mexico, and Utah. They don't live in wigwams but in "hogans," octagonal (eight-sided) houses made of mud, stone, and wood. The door faces to the east to greet the rising sun and belongings are arranged in a special way: bedding in the west, tools and utensils in the south, and medicines in the north.

In Navajo culture, songs and chants are recited from memory and performances can go on for nine days without a mistake being made. Navajo children soon learn to keep lots of information in their memories.

It seems anything the Navajos do, they do well. They make beautiful rugs and blankets, and silver and turquoise jewelry. Wool for weaving is colored with dyes made from desert plants. They grind colored rocks and minerals into fine powder and drop them onto the sand to form beautiful sand paintings. Very fine straight lines can be made in this way. These sand paintings were used in healing ceremonies and were always destroyed at sunset. Today the Navajo make framed sand paintings to sell to tourists.

Secret messages

Have you ever tried to crack a coded message? A code is a way of sending a message, often secretly, so that only those who know the code will be able to understand it. Codes can be written, spoken, or signalled. The Morse code, a mixture of dots and dashes, can be used in any of these ways. Semaphore is a signalled code in which flags are held in each hand and moved to different positions for each letter of the alphabet.

A spoken code can be a language which only those sending and receiving the message can understand. During the Second World War the Americans used Navajo soldiers to send radio messages in their own language, which is very difficult for anyone else to understand. They sent more than five hundred messages without a single mistake and the enemy was never able to break the code.

Good and bad spirits

The old beliefs of the Navajo are taught to them through stories, songs, and ceremonies. The spirits they believe in can be bad or good, so they find it hard to imagine a God who is only good. They fear witches, and use medicine and magic to try to protect themselves from bad spirits, witchcraft, and life's problems. Families sing special "protection" songs to try to get good crops and increase their sheep and cattle.

One out of every thirteen of the 200,000 Navajos are Christians. Many put their trust in Jesus after the Navajo Bible was printed in 1986. It had taken forty years to translate. A blind Navajo man, Geronimo Martin, read an English Braille Bible with his fingers. Braille is a system of writing for blind people in which raised dots are "read" by touch. While Geronimo read, he translated aloud into Navajo, and his wife recorded his words. Isn't it wonderful that a blind man was able to give his own people God's Word?

A few years ago a Navajo woman went to Finland to tell the Lapp people about Jesus and this has encouraged other Navajo Christians to become missionaries as well.

N stands for Navajos, who helped in the war, By their excellent memories trained in their lore.

You can pray for the Navajos

1 Dear Lord, please help many Navajos to read and understand their own Bible.

2 Help Navajo pastors and preachers to explain your truth to those who are still worshiping spirits.

3 Show them that you are not just the "white man's God," but Lord of all the earth.

4 Help Navajo young people not to get into bad habits like getting drunk and gambling, but to accept you and the happiness and peace you give.

5 Send Christian workers to show Navajo children that you love them and can take away their fears.

6 Just as some Navajo men bravely sent out messages in the war, make Navajo people spread your message in America and other countries.

7 Please send Christians to all the Indians of North and South America who have not believed in you.

WORLD MAP

Countries which are featured in this book are coloured orange on the map.

People groups which are featured in the book are coloured red on the map.

NORTH AMERICA

NAVAJOS

HAITI

VENEZUELA

QUECHUA

CHILDREN OF
THE STREETS

SOUTH AMERICA

QUECHUA

GYPSIES

EUROPE ROMANM

EUSKALDUNAK ALBANIA

GR

RIFF

AFRICA

WOLOF
JOLAS DOGON CHAD

LOBI

VAGLA

OVAMBO
ZIMB

HERERO

SAN

Z
LESOTH
XHO

PRAY
FOR THE WORLD

OMAN

WHERE OIL HAS REPLACED FRANKINCENSE

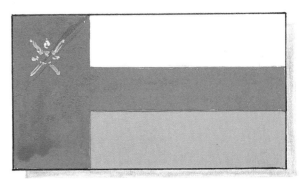

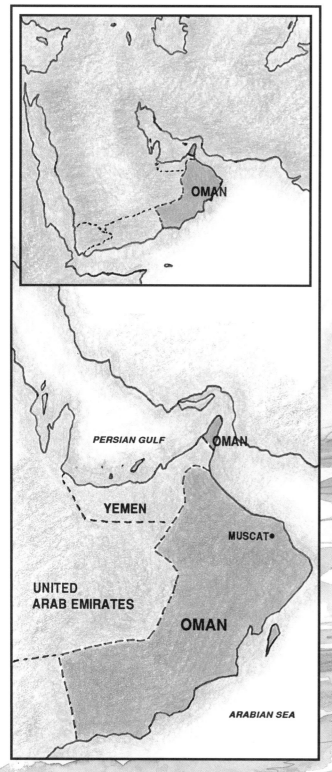

Oman is twice as large as the UK but has only one and a half million people. They are all Arabic-speaking Muslims, but are a surprising mixture. Different Arab clans, Indians, Baluch (see page 14), and Africans have been mixed together over the years to form the Omani nation.

Cut in two by the United Arab Emirates, the northern peninsula stretches out into the Arabian Gulf in a line of razor-sharp mountain peaks, some a mile high. From this peninsula,

Oman protects twenty thousand ships a year that pass in and out of the Gulf. Southern Oman, which is much larger, is full of mountains and stony plateaus, edged by sea and desert.

In ancient times the export of copper and

O

for Oman, an oil–rich state; The land of the palm, the pearl, and the date.

frankincense made Oman rich. In the Middle Ages Oman's ships sailed down the East African coast and across the Indian Ocean as far as China, trading in gold, ivory, iron and slaves.

Amazing canals

Sometimes we think the West is the most developed part of the world, but three thousand years ago an amazing network of underground irrigation canals was built in Oman. Called *falaj*, some were 9.3 miles long and 394 feet deep.

Muscat, the capital of Oman, has twin "fairytale" forts built in the cliffs. An earlier ruler and his two rebellious sons bombarded each other across the harbor

Frankincense.

from these forts. There are more than one thousand forts in the country.

By the middle of the last century Oman's wealth had declined. Even when oil was discovered in 1964 the ruler, Sultan Sa'id, was slow to use this new

wealth to modernize his country. Many Omanis went abroad and those left behind became discontented. Eventually Sultan Qaboos took control from his father in 1970 and told his people: "Oman in the past was in darkness . . . but a new dawn will rise."

In some ways that has come true. In 1970 Oman had just one hospital and three schools. Today there are fourteen hospitals, over 450 schools, modern ports and airports, new industries and color TV.

Christians are praying that another kind of darkness in Oman will disappear – the darkness in the lives of people who don't know Jesus. Because missionaries

built the first hospital, clinics, and schools, they are greatly respected in Oman, but they long to see Jesus loved by the Omani people. In spite of this loving service by missionaries, only about forty Omanis have ever become Christians. Muslims who decide to follow Jesus will almost certainly be persecuted by their families, friends, and the authorities.

In addition to the missionaries working in health care and education, there are other Christians from overseas working in regular jobs in Oman and wanting to tell Omanis about Jesus.

You can pray for Oman

1 Lord Jesus, please give Christians from overseas who work in Oman opportunities to meet Omanis and tell them about you.

2 Help Christians in the West to make friends with Omani students studying in their countries and show them your love.

3 Thank you for the Bible in Arabic. Help Omanis to want to read it so that they may understand that you are the only way to the true God.

4 Please give peace and joy to Omani Christians whose lives are not easy. Give them courage to speak about their faith in you.

5 Help Muslims as they go to prayers in their mosques to come to know the true God.

6 Help Christians to write books in Arabic for children, which will explain to them who you are and what you have done for them.

7 Send Arab Christian leaders to tell their people about you so they can clearly understand how their sins can be forgiven.

OVAMBO
OF NAMIBIA

WHERE LIONS PREY ON SEALS AND PENGUINS

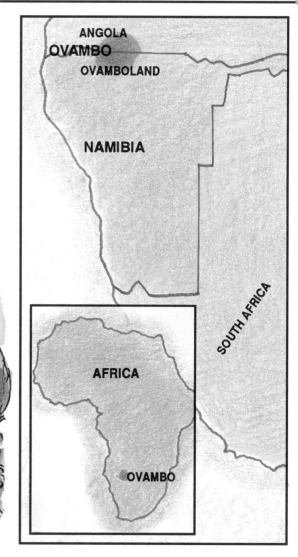

ANGOLA
OVAMBO
OVAMBOLAND

NAMIBIA

SOUTH AFRICA

AFRICA

OVAMBO

Namibia's beaches are extremely hot, but the seas are icy. The cold Antarctic water that flows up the West coast of Africa brings seals and penguins onto the beaches, where they become food for hungry lions!

Much of the country is harsh desert, and the few rivers only flow after occasional rainstorms. Ovamboland in the north is flat and sandy. Because more rain falls there than in the rest of Namibia many people live in Ovamboland.

Namibia became independent from South Africa in 1989 after more than twenty years of war. Most of the ruling party are now Ovambos. They have a difficult job: to resettle refugees, to rebuild their war-torn country and to make a society that is honest and fair to all its peoples.

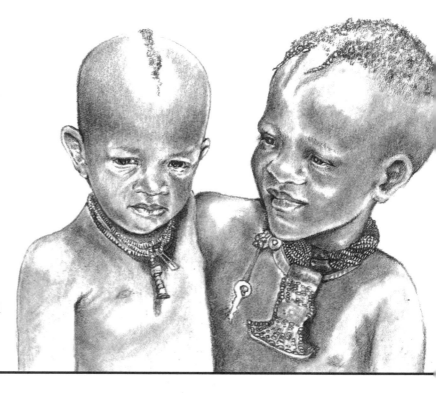

O for Ovambo, who raided for slaves, But now spread the news that Jesus Christ saves!

Filled with joy

The Ovambos are the largest tribe in Namibia. Long before white men arrived they made tools, ornaments, and weapons from iron and copper. They were animists (see page 114) who worshiped their ancestors, believing the Creator God wasn't interested in their needs. They were filled with joy when missionaries came and told them that the Creator God has reached out in love to them through Jesus. Many became Christians and they have sent missionaries to other countries.

Breakdown!

Emmanuel Heita, now an Ovambo evangelist, remembers those days well. He used to go out with his father to capture people to sell as slaves. One day a mission truck broke down outside his school. There were very few motor mechanics in Ovamboland, but one was at Emmanuel's school. While the mechanic repaired the truck the evangelists held a meeting for the children and Emmanuel heard about Jesus for the first time. He couldn't forget what he had heard and that night, sitting under a tree, he prayed that Jesus would forgive him for all the wrong things he had done.

Later he visited schools all over South Africa, playing his accordion and singing. Hundreds of children became Christians in meetings where he spoke. Two of his six children are twins who wouldn't have been allowed to live before Jesus changed the hearts of his people – twins used to be considered bad luck and were killed at birth.

Daydreaming

Toiva, an Ovambo boy, sat dreaming on the floor at Oshakati High School. With sixty children in his class, there were not enough desks, chairs, or books to go around. He looked longingly out of the broken windows, wishing he could be with his father's cattle, or setting bird traps or making cars and planes out of wire. Refugee children returning from the nearby countries of Angola and Zambia had made his school horribly crowded.

Toiva lives in a compound in which each of the twenty-five grass-thatched huts can be fenced off by barricades of sticks. The compound is built on slightly raised ground because the area floods after the January and February rains. Toiva and his friends love splashing about in the shallow flood water, which also attracts thousands of birds and wild animals.

You can pray for the Ovambo

1 Dear Lord, help Ovambo people who suffered during the war to settle down in their homes again and to find peace in you.

2 Help those who hurt others during the years of war to be sorry for what they did and ask for your forgiveness.

3 Help the country's leaders not to take revenge on people who fought against them. Help them to serve others rather than try to get rich themselves.

4 May the many Ovambo people with no jobs turn to you for help and not become thieves or troublemakers.

5 Show Christians different ways of helping refugees and unemployed people to earn a living.

6 Send Ovambo men and women to Bible school so they can learn how to bring others to know you.

7 Show the children from Christian homes that they must trust you and ask you into their lives for themselves.

PAPUA NEW GUINEA

AN UNTAMED LAND

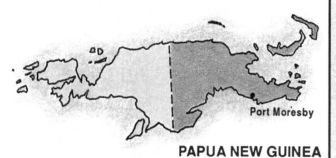

PAPUA NEW GUINEA

Port Moresby

PAPUA NEW GUINEA

AUSTRALIA

NEW ZEALAND

Papua New Guinea (PNG for short) and Irian Jaya form two halves of the world's second largest island. Steep mountains, fast-flowing rivers, and tropical jungle make it difficult for tribes in separate valleys to meet each other, so they speak many different languages. In PNG alone there are over seven hundred languages.

As roads and runways for aircraft have been built, tribes have become less isolated. When they meet they need a common language, so a form of Pidgin English has developed in which people from all the tribes can speak to each other. It is called "Tok Pisin" meaning "talk Pidgin."

"Tribes were always using witchcraft and fighting one another," said Joshua Damoi, head of the Christian Leaders' College in PNG. "But the good news of Jesus has helped our people to stop quarrelling and to work together. Of course Satan has still been trying to spoil the peace. There is rebellion and crime in different areas. However, now we have a specially strong weapon to fight back for God."

P

for Papua New Guinea, with peoples diverse; Many still fear the sorcerer's curse.

Spirit attack!

John, a missionary in PNG, had a haircut. He didn't pick up all the hair. His friend Aiyako was worried. "If you leave any hair on the ground, witchdoctors will use it to curse you," he warned.

"Watch out!" he said later. "You are near a spirit place and you will be poisoned."

When they were eating with people of another tribe he whispered, "Don't leave food on your plate. It may be used to attack us through the spirits."

Aiyako is full of fear. He

believes illnesses and accidents are caused by the spirits, and there are thousands of others like Aiyako who think like this. The Bible tells us that if we fear God – that means having a respectful trust in him – we needn't be afraid of anything else.

A new weapon

The "weapon" Joshua meant is the newly-translated Tok Pisin Bible. He said, "Many politicians think they have the answer to our problems, but they are wrong! The answer to our problems will come from people who read the Bible and let its message live in their hearts and guide their lives."

Thousands of missionaries have gone to PNG. Years ago some were killed and even eaten by the tribespeople they went to. Missionaries translated books of the Bible and brought health care, education, and the good news about Jesus to nearly every tribe. Sometimes whole villages became Christians! Although this seems wonderful, there is a danger that some, carried along with the crowd, didn't really turn away from doing wrong. Today many say they are Christians but still practice witchcraft and spiritworship.

Christian leaders are praying that the Bible and Christian films in Tok Pisin will make a difference to those who do not yet know Jesus.

You can pray for Papua New Guinea

1 Lord Jesus, please help Joshua Damoi and the students at the Christian College to live lives that please and honor you.

2 Thank you for the Tok Pisin Bible. Please help those who read it to stop doing wrong and find new life in you.

3 Help people to trust in you as they watch Christian films in Tok Pisin.

4 Set Christians free from the power of witchcraft and spirits.

Help them to know and love you and not to be afraid.

5 Fill evangelists with your Holy Spirit to teach men, women, and children clearly and lovingly about your truth.

6 Use evangelists and missionaries to translate the Bible into many more of PNG's languages.

7 Help whole families to have faith in you so that children can learn to trust and serve you when they are small.

71

PARSEES

THE WORLD'S FIRST CONSERVATIONISTS

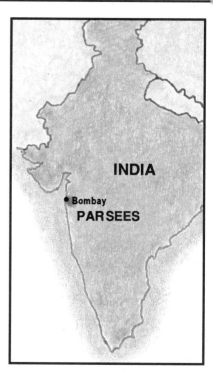

INDIA

Bombay
PARSEES

Homi was getting nervous as his seventh birthday approached, but his twin sister Fremmy was looking forward to it. On their birthday they would be taking part in an important religious ceremony in which they would become true Parsees. To prepare for this special day they were learning the beliefs of Zoroastrianism.

Homi was taking this very seriously indeed. They would promise to have good thoughts, words, and actions, and always to choose good rather than evil. They were taught that after death the good soul enters the house of eternal light, song, and purity, while the bad soul is sent to the house of impurity and darkness.

Homi truly wanted to be good but however hard he tried, angry thoughts still came into his mind. Sometimes he was rude to his mother or quarreled with Fremmy. He hoped the ceremony would change him inside so that he could be really good.

Zoroastrianism is practiced today by the seventy thousand Parsees who live in Bombay in India. They came originally from Fars, a province of Iran, fleeing from Muslims who were persecuting them. Although the Parsees are only a tiny group out of Bombay's ten million people, they have started over a thousand charities for the poor and needy of other races and faiths. Most Parsees are well-educated and rich, so there are not many needy people in their own group.

> **P** stands for Parsees, who live in Bombay; Their ancient religion they still keep today.

Special clothes

On their birthday, Homi and Fremmy were dressed in undershirts of soft white linen, called *sudreh.* A sacred cord, the *kushti,* made from seventy-two threads of lamb's wool, was tied around each of their waists. Then they prayed for help to keep the faith. The *kushti* is never taken off, but is retied five times a day when prayer is said.

No one except a Parsee may be a Zoroastrian. They do not share their beliefs with others, and even a person marrying a Parsee may not become one. Very few Parsees have ever become Christians. To be a Zoroastrian is part of their culture.

Some years ago a wealthy Parsee did become a Christian and a strong witness for Jesus,

Towers of silence

Parsees believe that as well as being pure and good themselves they must keep the air, earth, fire, and water pure too. Even their dead are not allowed to pollute the earth. When someone dies the body is taken to a tall "tower of silence" and laid on a sloping platform where vultures come and pick the bones clean. The bones

then slide down into a central well, disintegrate, and are absorbed by the earth. This concern for the environment began thousands of years before the rest of the world realized the need for conservation.

but a young girl who showed interest was severely scolded by her family and forbidden to have any further contact with

Christians. They are a kind and proud people who need to know the truth about Jesus.

You can pray for the Parsees

1 Dear Lord, please show Parsee children like Fremmy and Homi that they can only truly live good lives when you change their hearts.

2 Thank you for all the good things the Parsees do. Send Christians to show them your wonderful love and care for the world.

3 Help Parsees to realize that you died on the cross to make us clean inside, and only you can make us pure and holy.

4 Help Parsees to see that they can only pray to God the Father through Jesus.

5 Help many Parsees believe in you, in spite of the difficulties, and to see that the world they care for was made by you.

6 Bring Parsees in other parts of the world – whether doctors, businessmen, lawyers, or engineers – into contact with Christians who can explain clearly about Jesus.

7 Help Christians to want to share your truths with Parsees, and show them ways to do it.

QATAR

THE THUMB OF THE ARABIAN GULF

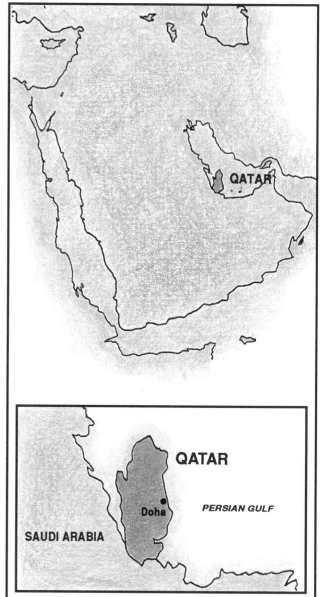

QATAR

QATAR

SAUDI ARABIA

Doha

PERSIAN GULF

No believers?

Young evangelists in a Western capital spoke excitedly to their team leader. "We've been talking to a man from the country of Qatar. Do you know anything about it?"

"Let's look it up in the book *Operation World*," he suggested. "Wow! It says that there are no known Qatari believers! We must pray for that man –

he could be the first."

The evangelists did not realize the suffering their new friend Ahmed (not his real name) would go through when he gave up Islam and asked Jesus into his life. His dearly-loved wife divorced him, his children were taken away and he was not allowed to return to his country.

On the map you can see Qatar sticking out like a thumb into the Arabian Gulf. It is an Arab country with only about 300,000 people, and the ruling Sheikh chooses his government ministers mainly from his own large family. Although he does not have to explain his actions to anyone, the Sheikh must keep Islamic law and consider the opinions of the Muslim religious leaders.

Once Qatar's main trade items were pearls and guano, a kind of manure produced by sea

birds that makes very good fertilizer. Oil was found in 1940, and later the largest reserves of natural gas in the world were discovered under the sea nearby. Since that discovery an airport has been built near the fast-growing port of Doha, Qatar's capital, and the country is so wealthy that the average family owns five cars!

Because it is so hot, attractive experimental farms use greenhouses that keep plants cool, not warm! Water shortages and the high cost of removing salt from

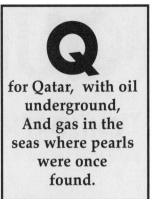

Q for Qatar, with oil underground, And gas in the seas where pearls were once found.

sea water mean that very little land can be farmed.

Thousands of people from other countries work in Qatar, so only one in three of those living there are true Qataris. The five thousand Britons are made to feel at home although the way they dress often upsets the local people. They are not allowed to hold Christian services or celebrate Christmas, but they do have their own newspaper, radio, and TV channels.

Qatari boys wear *thaubs* (white ankle-length shirts), sandals, and embroidered caps. As they get older the caps are covered with headcloths and kept in place by *agals* (thick black bands of twisted wool). Although allowed more freedom than girls, boys are constantly under their fathers' watchful eyes, and disobedience, bad marks, or failure to say the Muslim prayers can result in a beating.

Boys must help their father entertain guests in the *majlis*, a room set apart for male visitors. From the age of six they serve guests with coffee and must be perfectly quiet, not speaking unless spoken to. Older boys, wanting more freedom, like to speed about in cars in the desert and hold drinking parties, which are illegal. Many are afraid of the future, of failing their exams, and of punishment by God or their parents because of their bad habits. Islam demands obedience from everyone to its laws but cannot give people the power to keep them.

You can pray for Qatar

1 Lord, please help Christians in other lands to make friends with Qatari students and to show them your love.

2 Use each Arabic Bible and New Testament taken into Qatar to bring a Qatari person to know you.

3 Help Qatari women and girls, who have so little freedom, to know that you love and care for them.

4 Send Christians to work in Qatar in ordinary jobs and to show your love to everyone they meet.

5 As Qataris pray in their mosques show them that they cannot please the true God without knowing you.

6 Work a miracle by bringing the Sheikh and religious leaders to hear about you, to listen to your Word, and have the courage to accept you.

7 Please show us how to get the good news of your love to the world's many Muslims.

QUECHUA

CHILDREN OF THE INCAS

Scissor dancing

One day fourteen-year-old Garivay Timoteo, who is a Quechua, thought he heard the Devil telling him to dance "three feet in the air." He jumped and to his amazement he danced and leapt with energy far greater than his own. That day Garivay sadly entered into a pact with the Devil to perform a dance called the "scissor dance." The pact was a serious thing, as the Devil makes great demands on his dancers. First they must dance for days at a time, which leaves them exhausted. Then they must sew a violin string through their lip, and play a violin dangling from it.

"The Devil gave me a new name and told me what costume to wear," said Garivay proudly. Poor Garivay doesn't know that the Devil is the thief Jesus talked about in John's Gospel chapter 10 verse 10, who comes to "steal and kill and destroy." Nor does he know that Jesus is the Good Shepherd, who came to give us a wonderful new life that will last forever.

Descended from Incas

The ten million Quechua people of Peru are descended from the Incas. When the Spaniards arrived in South America in the sixteenth century, the Inca Empire spread from Ecuador to Chile, more than two thousand miles. The Incas built massive agricultural terraces, great palaces and temples, and a network of roads and cities. The emperor, or Inca, was supposed to be the son of the sun, and the Inca people believed themselves to be children of the sun and moon. When the Spaniards arrived, two brothers were quarrelling over who should be the next Inca, so the invaders were able to conquer the Incas quickly with just a small army.

Though their land is rich, many Quechuas are poor. Their gold and silver were stolen by the Spanish invaders. Many struggle to make a living on the high terraces of the cold Andes

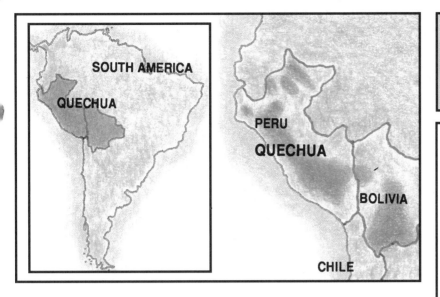

You can pray for the Quechua

1 Lord Jesus, please help Christians to show Quechua children like Garivay that your power is greater than the Devil's.

2 Help the Quechuas to understand that you are the Good Shepherd, and the Devil is wicked and not to be worshiped and obeyed.

3 Make the Quechua people stronger and wiser than their Inca ancestors, with strength and goodness that only come from knowing you.

4 Help Christians living where guerillas are fighting to trust you to protect them.

5 Help people who think they are Christians, but still go to spirit priests, to get to know you for themselves.

6 Show Christians how they can help those who are ill and poor, by providing them with food and care and teaching them your love.

7 Thank you for the new Quechua Bible. Please help those who read it to understand and obey your Word.

mountains. Others, with no land to farm, try to find jobs in the city slums. Sometimes they are in danger from guerillas called "The Shining Path," who have killed thousands of people in bombings and terrorist attacks.

The Quechua pay spirit priests who they believe can help them in their illnesses and problems. Many say they belong to the Roman Catholic Church, but are still trapped by their old spirit religion.

More than twenty different Quechua languages are spoken. Romulo Saune helped translate the first complete Bible in a Quechua language. As a little boy he cared for his family's sheep. Because he put his life in danger for the sheep, Romulo loves the verses in the Bible about Jesus, the Good Shepherd, who gave his life for us. He wants all his people to know the Good Shepherd for themselves.

ROMANIA

FREE AT LAST

The Romanian countryside is beautiful with high mountain passes, dramatic gorges, rolling plains, and thick forests. The river Danube forms much of Romania's southern border and wolves and bears still roam the mountains. Summers are very hot but short and winters bitterly cold, sometimes making the Danube freeze for several months. Romania once sent fine flour to French pastry-cooks, and wine all over the world. A wonderful place to live until a dictator appeared on the scene!

Nicolae Ceausescu ruled Romania for twenty-four years as a Communist dictator. He was cruel and called himself the Sacred Word, Saint, Savior, and Chosen One. He was surrounded by secret police and gave top jobs to his own family. He built secret passages under his fortress-like palace, where he hid many

weapons. At last in 1989 his desperate countrymen rose up and defeated him. In the end he had no place to hide.

Ceausescu bought many luxuries for himself, but to pay his country's debts he sold the fuel and food that his people badly needed to other countries. Life was hard and people had to stand in line for everything. Old and sick people and abandoned children were treated so badly that the whole world was shocked when they found out how they lived. Villagers were taken from their homes and put in ugly, badly-built blocks of flats so that their land could be made into big farms owned by the government. It was planned to destroy 7,000 villages in this way.

Nicolae Ceausescu.

Revolution!

The arrest of a pastor called Laszlo Tokes in November 1989 led to Ceausescu's downfall. Tokes bravely spoke out when villages were destroyed and Christians persecuted. Police confiscated his ration book, so he couldn't buy food or fuel. Church members weren't allowed to take him food. He and his wife were beaten by the secret police, and the windows of their church and home were smashed.

Thousands of church members and their neighbors gathered in the main square of Tokes' home town of Timisoara to protest, shouting "Down with Ceausescu and Communism!" When soldiers refused to shoot the demonstrators, the secret police drove tanks into the crowd. The army joined the people against Ceausescu, who was finally overthrown on Christmas night 1989.

For many years Christians in Romania were picked on, imprisoned, and even killed for believing in God. Although there is now more freedom, many believers are still afraid and don't know who to trust. Since the revolution at least a thousand churches have been started. There have also been Christian radio and TV programs. When "Superbook," the Bible in cartoons, was shown on TV, thirty thousand children wrote in each day asking for books and Bibles. Through watching this program, both children and adults have found Jesus. Many Romanians still do not know that only Jesus can give them peace and joy.

R

for Romania, hurt and forlorn, Where many new Christians are now being born.

You can pray for Romania

1 Lord Jesus, give Romania a government that will rule wisely and fairly and give Christians freedom to worship and tell others about you.

2 Thank you for brave men like Pastor Tokes. Give him and all church leaders in Romania your strength to teach and care for others.

3 Send your Holy Spirit to help Christians in Romania to forgive, love, and trust one another.

4 Provide Bibles and Christian books to teach Christians more about their faith and bring more Romanians to believe in you.

5 Help Christians from Romania and other countries to show your love to the thousands of abandoned children and old people who have not been cared for.

6 Help Christian children and young people to face the many changes in Romania, and to tell their friends about you.

7 Show Christians in the West how to help the Romanian churches grow and become strong.

RIFF

BERBERS OF THE ATLAS MOUNTAINS

Jamina, a ten-year-old Riff girl from north Morocco, was helping her mother prepare for the feast of Eid el-Kabir. On this day Muslims sacrifice and then eat a sheep to celebrate Abraham's willingness to sacrifice his son Ishmael, and God's provision of a sheep to sacrifice instead. Are you thinking that the son was Isaac, not Ishmael? You're right! Muslims believe that Abraham took Ishmael (from

The original people of North Africa were called Berbers. They were conquered in the 8th century by Arabs who have ruled North Africa ever since. The twenty-one million Berber people speak sixty-eight different languages and dialects. The Riff are one of the three main groups of Berber people, and many of them live in the Atlas mountains of Morocco.

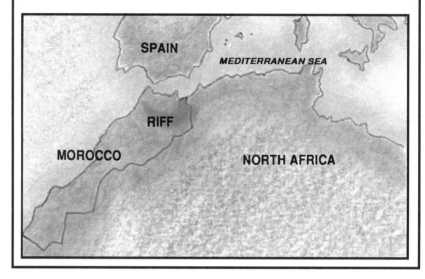

whom all Arab peoples are descended) – even though it doesn't say that in the Koran. You can read the Bible story in Genesis 22.

M.Filidis

Jamina removed the grit from the lentils and soaked them ready for cooking. Then she kneaded dough to make bread. Her mother was cooking the flat round loaves, made without yeast, on a large plate over the fire. Her hands were tough and hard from working in the fields.

Jamina's birth

For perhaps the hundredth time she told the story of Jamina's birth. "I wanted a baby so much. Your father was looking for another wife because I couldn't have a baby. I cried and didn't know what to do. Then my mother took me to a saint's tomb and I was told to jump three times through the tomb window. Soon I was pregnant. You were my beautiful baby, Jamina!"

Jamina's father had prepared the sheep. Her brother and sister, who had few toys, were having great fun blowing up the sheep's lungs like a balloon and shouting excitedly. Jamina was looking forward to eating meat again; mostly their food was bread and olive oil, and sometimes lentils or fresh sardines.

Jamina was proud of her father, who worked across the sea in Spain and had returned for the feast. Other Riff men married a second wife on their visits to Europe, smoked and drank, and had no money to bring back for their families in the mountains. But not Jamina's father – he loved his children and did everything he could for them.

The loaves smelled delicious.

R for the Riff who on radio waves Could be hearing the news that Jesus Christ saves.

Jamina liked their flat, round shape. Mohammed, her brother, was glad of the holiday because he hated school. Sometimes he was beaten and jeered at for mistakes when reciting the Koran, and he often came home crying. Jamina, like most Riff girls, had only been to school for three years. She was needed at home to fetch water and wood, care for her baby sister, whom she carried on her back, sweep the house, and work in the fields.

Almost all Berbers are Muslims; among the one and a half million Riff only about forty have been baptized as Christians. These came to know Jesus through Berber and Arabic radio broadcasts, or through Bible correspondence courses sent through the mail. One man who couldn't read or write asked his brother to help him with a correspondence course, and as a result both asked Jesus into their lives.

You can pray for the Riff

1 Dear Lord, please send Christians who are good at learning languages to go and work among the Berber people, and take them your message of love.

2 Help many Berbers to listen to Christian broadcasts and to study Bible correspondence courses.

3 Help those who mark correspondence courses to answer students' questions carefully and wisely so they may come to believe in you.

4 Show the Berbers that honoring dead saints is not pleasing to God, even if they seem to get what they ask for.

5 Help new Christians to be sorry for the times in the past when they asked dead saints for help.

6 May Christians help children to learn Bible passages by heart, just as they learned the Koran.

7 Make Riff Christians so joyful that their Muslim friends will want to know you too.

SRI LANKA

ISLAND OF BEAUTY AND BATTLE

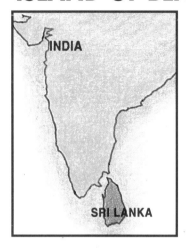

Golden beaches

Sri Lanka, just south of India, is a beautiful sunny island, with many golden palm-fringed beaches. It is very fertile, producing tea, rubber, spices, coconuts, and tropical fruits. Fish caught in the sea are laid to dry on saffron yellow cloths on the sand. Buffalo carts, tiny three-wheeled taxis, bicycles, cars, and ancient buses fill the busy streets.

About seventeen million people live in Sri Lanka. The twelve million local people, who are called Sinhalese, are mostly Buddhist; the three million Tamils, whose ancestors came from India, are mainly Hindu; and there are one million Muslim Moors, as well as several other smaller races.

Since 1980 violence has disrupted the country.

A puzzling move

Jayanthi couldn't understand it! Her parents had left their lovely home in the suburbs of Colombo, Sri Lanka's capital, and had come with a few belongings to a poor village many miles from the city. Now her clever father and mother had to learn how to plaster the walls of their hut and to thatch the roof with coconut palms.

Her parents, Lalith and Hiranthi, saddened by the violence in their country, had prayed and fasted, asking God to send peace and end the suffering of the many refugees, orphans, and poor people they saw daily. God answered their prayers by telling them to do something about it themselves! Lalith gave up his medical career and Hiranthi gave up her law practice to live in a simple village so that they could understand the needs of the people and tell them about Jesus.

Some Tamils believe that the government, mainly made up of Sinhalese, has treated them unfairly. In the north and east of the island Tamil guerillas are fighting government forces, trying to make a separate country for themselves.

Elsewhere there are Sinhalese Communists who want to overthrow the government and share out Sri Lanka's riches more widely. They have murdered officials and politicians and have even encouraged young school children to demonstrate, to throw stones at cars and buses, and put anti-government posters on walls. Many of the leaders of this movement have been

killed, or put into detention camps or prisons. Lalith and his helpers give medical care, food, and clothes, and bring words of hope and healing to such prisoners.

Christians help
Other Christians in Sri Lanka are giving aid, Bibles, and books to refugees fleeing the fighting. Some of these refugees are trusting Jesus, realizing he is the only One who can help and give them peace.

Children need help the most. Some have lost parents in the fighting and live on the streets. Some are involved in the violence, while others have to work long hours in unhealthy, dangerous

jobs for very little money.

Once called a pearl because of its shape, today Sri Lanka reminds people of a tear. Only Jesus, through the power of his Holy Spirit, can bring back peace and prosperity to this island.

S

for Sri Lanka, whose beauty and sun Are spoiled by strife and the sound of a gun.

You can pray for Sri Lanka

1 Lord Jesus, please break the power of Satan in Sri Lanka and help people of all races to see that you are the answer to their problems.

2 Give strength to Lalith and other Christians as they work in villages, refugee camps, and prisons.

3 Send Christians to preach in the many villages where you are not known.

4 Help Sri Lankan believers to write books explaining to Buddhists that you are the way, the truth, and the life.

5 Change the hearts of Buddhists, Hindus, and Muslims through the Holy Spirit so that as they hear the truth, and understand it they will believe it for themselves.

6 Send people filled with your love to care for children orphaned in the fighting or whose parents are unable to care for them.

7 Thank you for Sri Lankans who are turning to you because of the suffering in their land and are finding comfort and a new way of life.

A Buddhist temple in Sri Lanka.

SAN

TINY BUSHMEN OF THE KALAHARI DESERT

A hundred years ago a missionary named Frederick Arnot was traveling with African helpers through the Kalahari Desert in Botswana to reach the Zambezi River. Almost fainting from thirst, they struggled towards a water hole. They despaired when they found it was completely dry. Some were kneeling, others lay unconscious on the sand. None could go on without water.

From a distance a group of San Bushmen had seen them. They ran to the spot and began digging furiously, scooping up handfuls of sand. Their leader took several lengths of reed and slid them into the hole. Carefully he pushed the reeds, skillfully jointed together, into the ground. After sucking and blowing for some time he smiled – water!

He began to suck steadily on the reed, and as water slowly rose up the stem he spat it into a tortoise shell. Ten minutes later the shell was full. He gently poured this precious water over Arnot's tongue and down his throat until Arnot was able to swallow. For six hours the sweating Bushmen worked without pause to get water for the whole group. Then, without waiting for thanks, the Bushmen left as silently as they had come.

In those days the San Bushmen were hunted like wild animals by the surrounding peoples who wanted the Bushmen's land for themselves. How wonderful that, having received nothing but cruelty from others, they saved the lives of strangers. As a result of this Tinka, Arnot's chief guide, actually became a Christian as he saw how God had looked after them.

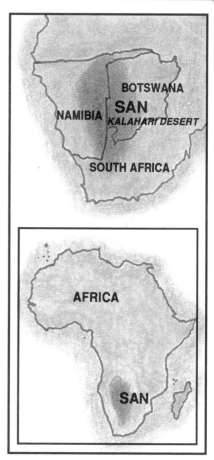

Poisoned arrows

The San Bushmen build shelters of branches, twigs, and grass to live in when they move about hunting wild animals and gathering roots and berries. They shoot animals with poisoned arrows and eat them the same day. The skin around their stomachs is wrinkled and able to stretch to hold a large amount of food so they can go without for long periods.

Once Bushmen roamed freely over Southern and East Africa. Beautiful rock paintings show their beliefs, the animals they hunted, and their way of life. Their places of safety from white men and other African tribes became fewer, so most had to give up their nomadic lifestyle and change to fit in with life on farms or in towns. The Botswana government is doing all it can to help them settle and to give them land rights, water, and education.

There are about thirty different San Bushman languages. Many of the words contain click sounds, made with the tongue against the teeth or roof of the mouth. One click is like the sound we make to

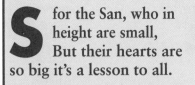

S for the San, who in height are small, But their hearts are so big it's a lesson to all.

urge on a horse, another the "tut tut" of disapproval. A mission called Language Recordings has put Bible talks on tape in some Bushman languages, and missionaries are telling them the good news of Jesus. Not all Bushmen have heard about Jesus, but some have decided to follow him.

You can pray for the San Bushmen

1 Dear Lord, please help the San Bushmen to realize they are under the power of Satan through their fear of the spirit world, and show them you can set them free.

2 Help the San Bushman leaders to hear about your love and forgiveness and to put their faith in you.

3 Help the Bushmen to change happily to life in the farms and modern towns without losing their gentle ways.

4 Send men and women to translate the Bible into all the Bushman languages.

5 Help Language Recordings workers to find scattered Bushman groups and make Christian tapes of all Bushman languages and dialects.

6 Help missionaries to love and understand these people so that Bushmen may realize how precious they are to you.

7 Bring Bushmen to faith in you, so that they can help other people as they helped Arnot long ago.

TURKEY

WHERE EAST MEETS WEST

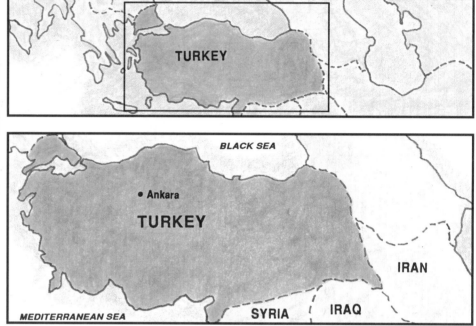

An invitation

Gul and her younger brother Ali were very excited. The previous day an unexpected note had dropped through the door of their home on the outskirts of a large city in Turkey. It was an invitation to meet two foreign friends of their older sister, Aysha, at a hotel in the city center.

They were also a little nervous. About three years earlier Aysha had shocked the whole family by telling them that she had become a believer in Jesus, something that is very unusual in Turkey. Then she surprised them even more by announcing that she was going to marry someone from America, and not a Turkish young man as her parents would have wanted. What would Aysha's friends be like?

Fortunately they had nothing to worry about. Debbie and Sue, who had sent them the note, were so friendly that Gul and Ali liked them at once. They were surprised how well their new friends spoke the Turkish language, and how much they seemed to enjoy living in Turkey.

Soon Ali was busy telling Sue about life at school and at home, while Gul and Debbie were talking quietly about more serious things. Gul told Debbie that she and her sister had talked many times about faith in Jesus, and that recently Gul had prayed and asked Jesus to forgive her sins.

When they said good-bye later that day, Gul and Ali promised to persuade their parents to invite Debbie and Sue to their home. Although they had been upset when Aysha stopped following Islam and became a Christian, they could also see that her faith had given her a new love and respect for them.

Picnics

Debbie and Sue were soon regular visitors to Gul and Ali's home, and sometimes they would take them on picnics into the mountains. Often one of them would be able to study the Bible with Gul, teaching her more about following Jesus.

Before long Gul and Ali's parents became interested in the message of the Bible too. They watched a video about the life of Jesus, and found it very moving. Father read right through Matthew's Gospel, and had a dream about Jesus dressed in shining robes. Mother wept as she understood more about God's love, and quietly started to give New Testaments to some of her friends.

Two continents

Just a small part of Turkey is in Europe, which ends at the western half of the large city of Istanbul. The other half, reached by ferry or bridge across a stretch of water called the Bosphorus, is in Asia.

Because the fifty-six million Turks are almost all Muslims, it is difficult for the few who love Jesus to tell others about him. Although the law does not forbid people becoming Christians, some Turkish Christians have been prevented from meeting together to worship God or have lost their jobs. Some have even been kept in prison for a while. It is difficult being a Christian in Turkey.

Fortunately many more families, just like Gul and Ali's, are taking an interest in Christianity. Several thousands of people are studying the Bible through correspondence courses, and Christians like Debbie and Sue are always ready to visit those who want to learn more.

You can pray for Turkey

1 Lord Jesus, please send Christians filled with your love to tell Turkey's Muslims about you.

2 Help churches near me adopt and pray for one of Turkey's seventy-three provinces. May there soon be at least one Christian in each province.

3 Strengthen the Turkish Christians who have been in prison for their faith in you, and fill them with your courage and joy.

4 Use the Turkish New Testament and Christian videos and books to show Muslims that you are the only way to God.

5 Help many more Turks to turn from everything they know is wrong and to believe that you died on the cross for them and rose again.

6 Break the power of Islam in Turkey and its control over people's lives.

7 Thank you for the modern version of the Turkish New Testament. Help those translating the Old Testament.

T stands for Turkey, where two continents meet; Folk from Asia and Europe are seen in the street.

TIBETANS

WHO STUCK OUT THEIR TONGUES TO SAY HELLO

A lost world

For centuries Tibet was like a lost world. The high Himalayan mountains surrounded it like a wall, and Tibet's leaders kept out all but a few traders from neighboring countries. The Buddhist religious leaders were also the political rulers. The officials and priests were treated like nobles but the ordinary people were serfs. They had to put out their tongues when they met the nobility, to show they did not have demons inside them that could cause harm!

From the age of five, thousands of boys entered lamaseries to become monks and learn the Buddhist scriptures. Discipline there was very strict.

The most important priest or "lama" in the land was the Dalai Lama, meaning Ocean of

Wisdom. He was said to be a god-king and lived in a magnificent palace, the Potala, in the capital city, Lhasa. The present Dalai Lama, Tenzin Gyatso, was born in 1935 in a simple farmhouse hundreds of miles from Lhasa. Tibetans believe that when a Dalai Lama dies his soul is "reborn" in a new-born baby. Soon after the death of a Dalai Lama, the search begins to find his successor, who has to be a child born within eighteen months of his death.

After his enthronement in the Potala, the Dalai Lama began religious studies. He was never allowed to leave the Potala, unless visiting another lamasery, so he would use binoculars to see what was happening outside. He would be able to see the pilgrims outside bowing down over and over again; small servant girls carrying wood and water and running errands; and richly dressed officials arriving at the Potala on horseback.

Then in 1950 the Chinese

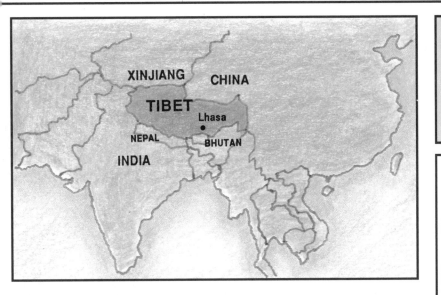

army invaded Tibet and within a few years the Dalai Lama was forced to flee to India, where he has lived ever since. Thousands of Tibetans were killed by the Chinese and thousands more fled to India and Nepal.

Lamaseries were burnt and destroyed along with the ancient Buddhist scriptures, and a Communist government was set up.

Breakthrough

Many Tibetans are still devoted to their god-king and want Tibet to be independent. Riots and demonstrations led by monks have been broken up by the Chinese with great force. However, the Chinese takeover of Tibet has brought some progress. Priests no longer have total power and most children are able to go to school. After centuries of spirit worship some Tibetans in India, Nepal, and Tibet are hearing the good news about Jesus and have become Christians.

You can pray for the Tibetans

1 Dear Lord, please bring Buddhism to an end in Tibet, so that fear of spirits and demons may never again rule the lives of the people.

2 May Western and Chinese Christians be free to travel all over Tibet with the good news of your love.

3 Send Tibetans who have become Christians in India and Nepal back to Tibet to tell their families and friends about you.

4 Show Tibetans that the Dalai Lama is only a man and not a god.

5 Show Tibetans that you care for them so much that you died on the cross to save them from their sins.

6 Help Tibetans to discover that you are the true "Ocean of Wisdom" and the King of kings.

7 Help Christians to write stories and books for Tibetan children so that they may learn about you.

UNITED ARAB EMIRATES

MORE FOREIGNERS THAN LOCALS

Once seven Arab sheikhs each ruled their own lands, called sheikhdoms or emirates, in the Arabian Gulf area. In 1972 they joined together to become the United Arab Emirates (or UAE for short) with the largest emirate, Abu Dhabi, as the capital city.

Money from oil, which is found in four of the emirates, has changed the country rapidly. Simple villages in the desert have become modern cities. Harbors, once the haunt of pirates, smugglers, and Arab dhows (trading boats) are now ports for huge oil tankers. The port of Jebil Ali in Dubai has room for over sixty ships. Six international airports in the UAE handle more than seven million passengers a year.

Oil and sand
Most of the UAE is hot, dry desert, but a little rain falls in the eastern mountains. Vegetables, dates, and limes are grown where the land is irrigated.

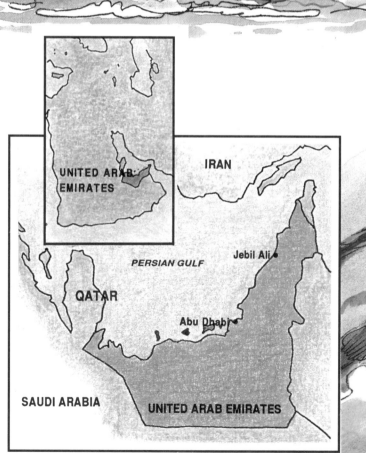

IRAN

UNITED ARAB EMIRATES

PERSIAN GULF

Jebil Ali

QATAR

Abu Dhabi

SAUDI ARABIA

UNITED ARAB EMIRATES

Money from the sale of oil has been spent on removing the salt from sea water so it can be used to irrigate crops, keep cattle, and beautify the cities with green parks and fountains.

More trade has brought thousands of immigrants and temporary workers from abroad, so only about twelve people out of every hundred are locals.

Everyone loves to watch camel races, and bullfights in which bulls wrestle with each other. Usually one quickly shows it is stronger and the other turns and runs, its owner hanging on to its tether! Some sheikhs hunt with falcons in the desert.

U
stands for the UAE, Where sheikhs have joined their territory.

When the UAE was a poor country, Christian missionaries provided the only medical care. Christian nurses and midwives saved many lives, and their love and concern are still remembered. Today modern hospitals and clinics are available to everyone, but the few remaining Christian medical centers are still popular because the love of Jesus is shown through the care given by the staff.

Girls and boys at home

As in many Muslim countries, some men have more than one wife, so children have the same father but may have a different mother. Boys are taught that they are more important than girls, and expect their sisters and mothers to wait on them. Many young men go to foreign lands to study, but girls may not leave the Emirates.

When children start school at about six or seven, boys and girls are separated. Boys play soccer and roam about with friends, but girls may only play in the garden or go visiting with their mothers. When they are nine, girls must wear black cloths on their heads in public, and at thirteen the black cloak and veil which all Muslim women wear in the street.

Fathers arrange marriages for their daughters, who are seldom, if ever, consulted. Some are even forced to marry as young as thirteen, if their husband's father is eager to get his hands on the dowry. They have little to look forward to on earth and no hope for the future, as even the best Muslims can never be sure God has forgiven their sins and accepted them.

British, Pakistani, Filipino, Indian, and Arab Christians working in the UAE are allowed to meet and worship as long as they don't tell Muslims about Jesus. A Pakistani was sent back to Pakistan for talking about Jesus to a Muslim, and other Christians have been imprisoned for the same crime.

You can pray for the UAE

1 Lord Jesus, please show the people of the Emirates that Islam can't save them from punishment for their sins, but you can.

2 Help Christians working in the UAE to speak wisely and powerfully about your love for Arab people.

3 Give skill to Christian nurses and midwives, and help patients to trust them enough to share their troubles with them.

4 Remind Christians in the West to invite students from the Emirates to their homes, to share their family life, and show them your love.

5 Make it possible for Muslim children living in the UAE to hear about your love.

6 Work through miracles, dreams, and visions to show Muslims your power, holiness, and truth.

7 Give those who trust you courage to stay loyal to you, even if they are badly treated because of their faith.

UZBEKS

WHO MAPPED THE STARS 500 YEARS AGO

Tashkent is the capital of Uzbekistan, part of the CIS (the old Soviet Union). The old Communist government stopped Russian and German Christians and Uzbeki Muslims living there from practicing their religion. They were not allowed to teach their beliefs in schools, mosques, or churches, and very few copies of the Bible or Koran were allowed. So young Uzbeks only know about Islam from the little they hear at weddings, birth ceremonies, and funerals.

Punished!

Ulugh, an eight-year-old Uzbek boy, arrived home from school in Tashkent to find his sister Rakhima sobbing, a cloth thrown over her head. "What's the matter?" he asked.

"Oh, Ulugh, some horrid men caught me as I was going to college, and shaved off my hair!" Rakhima pulled the cloth off her head to show him her bare scalp and then quickly covered it again.

"How awful, Rakhima. Why did they do it? Your leg's bleeding too."

"They said it was to punish me for not wearing my hair in long plaits as they think all Uzbek girls should. Then they cut my leg because they thought my skirt was too short. I'm afraid to walk in the street again, and I can't go to college with my head like this!"

When their parents returned home from work they were very upset about the attack. "It must have been Muslim fanatics. They want us to go back to the old ways," their father said.

U for the Uzbeks, who do not yet see The Savior who died that they may go free.

Secret Christians

Since Communism has collapsed in the old Soviet Union people are more free to follow their religious beliefs. But in Uzbekistan most Christian missionary work has to be done in secret because Islam is so strong there.

"If the fanatics think behaving like this is going to make us Muslims again, they're wrong!" Ulugh's father said angrily.

Rakhima agreed. "I don't want to wear a veil in the street, or marry an old man I don't like and have to get my husband's permission to leave the house."

"Is Islam bad, Daddy?" asked Ulugh. "What about the great Muslim Ulugh-Beg?" (Ulugh-Beg was a famous astronomer who built a great observatory five hundred years ago and discovered 1,018 stars.)

"No, Islam is not all bad, and we have had great Muslim builders and poets. But most Uzbeks couldn't even read and Islam did not give us much freedom. Your mother wouldn't be a teacher nor I a doctor if the Communists hadn't taken over our country."

"Communists have made mistakes too, but I don't want life to be like it was before," Ulugh's mother added.

"Many Uzbeks want to return to Islam," Ulugh's father sighed, "but I don't. I don't believe in God."

"Who made us then, and the birds, and the stars that Ulugh-Beg counted?" asked Ulugh, puzzled.

"You'll have to decide that for yourself! Off to bed now, and if there is a God, pray that Rakhima's hair may grow quickly!"

Uzbekistan is a troubled land. Most Uzbeks want to be Muslims again, but not as strictly as in the past. One million people have no jobs and the many cotton growers are paid too little for their hard work in the hot sun. Uzbeks need the peace and security that only Jesus can give but, out of eighteen million Uzbeks, only about thirty believe in Jesus.

You can pray for the Uzbeks

1 Dear Lord, help German and Russian Christians in Uzbekistan to tell Uzbeks about you.

2 Help Trans World Radio find Uzbek Christians who can make Christian programs in the Uzbek language.

3 May Christian missionaries not have to work in secret any longer.

4 Inspire Uzbek Christians to write leaflets and books that clearly show Muslims the truth about you.

5 Help Uzbek people, both atheists and Muslims, to search for the forgiveness and peace that only you can give.

6 Bring Uzbeks closer to you through reading the Uzbek New Testament, and help Christians to give away as many copies as possible.

7 Help the Uzbeks to be ready to believe your Word.

VENEZUELA

"LITTLE VENICE"

Venezuela, a modern country in South America, has more than twenty national parks, the highest waterfall in the world (the Angel Falls), miles of sandy beaches, mountains, plains, and tropical jungles. The capital, Caracas, and all the main towns have modern buildings. At the north end of Lake Maracaibo are some of the largest oilfields in the world. Nearby live the Goaro Indians. Their houses, raised on stilts above the lake, gave the country its name, Venezuela – "little Venice" – as the Italian city of Venice is also built on water.

Some people are very rich, but most are very poor. Thousands live in cramped houses made of corrugated iron, bits of wood, and plastic sheeting. The rich live in houses so grand that they need barred windows and doors, alarm systems, and fierce dogs to protect them.

V

for Venezuela, with rich and with poor; The poor's shack is plastic, the rich locks his door.

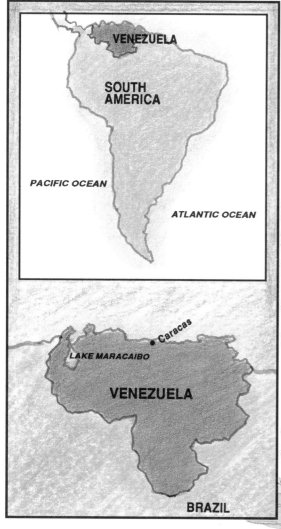

VENEZUELA

SOUTH AMERICA

PACIFIC OCEAN

ATLANTIC OCEAN

Caracas

LAKE MARACAIBO

VENEZUELA

BRAZIL

Video clubs

Recently some young people in Venezuela have gotten excited about their faith in Jesus. They belong to church clubs and tell their friends about him. Some are training to go abroad as missionaries. Special videos for children are being shown in Bible clubs and churches. Perhaps the children of Venezuela will bring their country to Jesus!

You can pray for Venezuela

1 Dear Lord, please do in Venezuela what you have done in the rest of South America.

2 Show people that promises to dead saints can't help them, but that you are alive today and can help them.

3 Help rich people to come to know you and to share their wealth with the poor.

4 Send Christians to the Yanomamo Indians, so that they may hear of you and come to trust in you.

5 Help thousands of children to hear your message of love and for-giveness.

6 Help people to under-stand that charms can't help them and that it is fool-ish and dangerous to trust in evil powers.

7 Help missionaries and local evangelists talk to the rich people about Jesus and not be afraid of their barred houses and fierce dogs.

Hammock beds

Many Venezuelans live in cities, but some live on the grassy plains. Here the people sleep in hammocks, which can be slung anywhere between two poles or hooks. Most Venezuelan children go to school, some starting when they are only three years old. Although edu-cation is free, poor chil-dren often leave school after only a few years.

The few thousand Yanomamo Indians live in the southeastern rain forests of Venezuela and over the border in Brazil. They are fierce and war-

like, and there is often fighting between them. They know little of the world beyond their thatched houses, small vegetable plots, and the wild pigs, monkeys, and plumed birds in the forest. When they count their language has words for only "one," "two," and "many."

The New Testament has been translated into their language, and some Christian recordings have been made for them. More missionaries are needed to tell these people about the love of Jesus, but sometimes the officials make it difficult for this to happen.

After Columbus

After Christopher Columbus discovered Venezuela in 1498 it was ruled by Spain. In 1830 it became independent but kept the Spanish language and the Roman Catholic religion. Almost everyone believes in God and Jesus, but it seems to make little difference to their lives. Getting a good job, staying healthy, and winning

money are so important that many make promis-es to dead saints to "bar-gain" for such things. At Easter everyone is sad because Jesus died, but few know that he rose from the dead to forgive them their sins. In other parts of South America millions have put their trust in Jesus, but very few have done this in Venezuela.

Sadly many people in Venezuela visit witches

to buy charms when they need help. Even big cities have shops selling magic – to make people fall in love, or give success in exams, for example. These charms rarely work, and they always bring the person using them under the power of evil spirits. The Bible warns against such things.

VAGLA

PEOPLE OF THE TALKING DRUMS

The fable of the drum

Once upon a time there was a Vagla man who kept getting lost while he was out hunting, so his young son spent a lot of time searching for him. One day when out searching for his father, the son reached a river where he heard drumming and singing. He listened carefully, wondering if his father was nearby.

A crocodile lying on the bank offered to take him out into the river to see who was drumming. From the crocodile's back the boy looked down into the water and saw people dancing to the drums.

"Have you seen my father?" the boy asked.

"No, he's not here," they replied, "but we'll help you. You can have our drums, and whenever your father is lost in the forest, you must beat them. Then he'll be able to find his way back to the village."

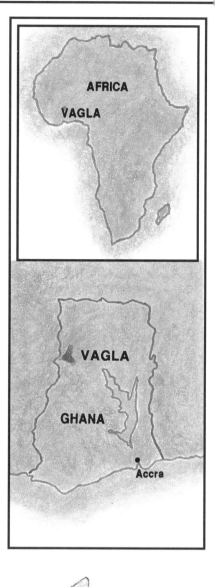

Never again did the boy have to search for his father. The drums sent such clear messages over long distances that the village elders began to use them for the whole village.

This fable was told by a Vagla chief to teach young people about the need to send clear messages. Vagla people use drums to send messages because their language is musical. If someone says a word in a high voice it means something different from saying it in a low voice. This makes it possible to beat out messages in musical notes so that everyone can understand what is being "said" by the drums.

The god Kiipo

The Vagla people live in north-west Ghana. There are only six thousand of them. They worship a god called Kiipo, hoping he will give them enough food and keep them safe from enemies and spirits. But worshiping Kiipo puts them under the power of evil spirits. Every village has its own priest to sacrifice chickens, sheep, or cattle to Kiipo.

Rooftop business

Villages consist of ten or more rectangular houses with courtyards, joined together under one roof. This strong flat roof is used as a street, and village life takes place up there. The Vagla men, wearing colorful cotton garments, meet on the rooftops to talk business. No one may sit or stand still on the ladders leading to the roof as the Vagla believe the spirits like to sit there.

Nearly all Vagla Christians are young men who still work with their fathers on the family farm. They don't earn any money, so they can't give much to pay a pastor's wages. Because their houses are linked together, anyone wanting to live or worship in a different way is noticed and persecuted. Relatives and village elders try to force new Christians to take part in the ceremonies and sacrifices to Kiipo.

Four Vaglas have been to Bible school and several more are training to be pastors. Men and women who can use fables, proverbs, and talking drums to teach others are needed to make God's message clear to the whole tribe.

V stands for Vagla, whose musical tongue Can be "spoken" by beats on an African drum!

You can pray for the Vagla

1 Lord Jesus, please help young Vagla Christians to be faithful to you and not join in worshiping Kiipo.

2 Show Vagla Christians how to help their pastors.

3 Thank you for the Vagla New Testament. Help people learning to read it to love your Word and obey it

4 Help Vagla Christians to write Christian stories, fables, and books to explain the Christian message to their people.

5 Help Vagla Christians to teach children how they can know you as their friend.

6 Show your power to the village elders and priests of Kiipo, so that they will turn away from idols to faith in you.

7 Help Vagla Christians want to share your good news with their neighbors, the Chakala people, so that they may trust in you too.

WESTERN SAMOA

A LAND FOUNDED ON GOD

Prayer time

"Please be quiet now, it's the time for prayer," the village lady whispered to her visitors from overseas. Her friends felt very embarrassed. They realized they had been talking at a time when everyone else in Western Samoa stops for prayer, a hymn, and a Bible reading, when the church bells ring at dusk each day.

Western Samoa, in the South Pacific Ocean, has two main islands and nine smaller ones. Sixty miles east lies American Samoa, a much wealthier island which is ruled by the USA. Although Western Samoa's people are poor, they are proud to be independent. Some young people are attracted to a richer way of life in American Samoa, New Zealand, and Australia.

Western Samoa is beautiful. Its fertile islands, formed by volcanos and surrounded by coral reefs, produce mangoes, coconuts, pineapples, and breadfruit (which grows on a tree but tastes somewhat like potatoes). The sea is rich in all types of fish, shellfish, and turtles. Sacks of sea urchins are collected, cracked open like eggs, and eaten raw. Houses called *fales* are built open to the breeze, and only in very bad weather are the canvas sides lowered.

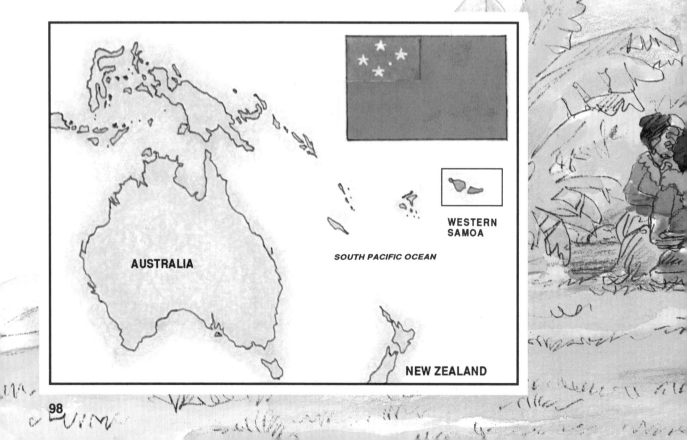

AUSTRALIA

SOUTH PACIFIC OCEAN

WESTERN SAMOA

NEW ZEALAND

Western Samoa

*a beautiful land,
Filled with
flowers and fruits,
blue lagoons and
white sand.*

Delicious feasts

The Samoans are very friendly and hold feasts where each delicious dish is announced before being placed before the guests. The food, wrapped in leaves, is cooked among hot stones. Often guests are decorated with turtle-shell combs, coral necklaces, and coconut-shell brooches, and given a *lapa lapa*, a skirt worn by both men and women. Strangely enough in church men wear shirts, ties, and jackets despite the heat, but have bare feet and wear *lapa lapas*, not trousers.

More than one hundred and sixty thousand people live in Western Samoa and most would say that they attend church and are Christians. Worship is lively with services twice during the week as well as on Sundays, and often there's an early-morning prayer meeting too. Sadly, in spite of all this, many people do not really know the Lord Jesus. It may be because some old Samoan customs and ceremonies that honor evil spirits are still followed.

In the 1800s missionaries from Samoa went all over the Pacific, filled with a great love for Jesus and God's Word. Now, for most Samoans, Christianity is just a part of their culture, like their feasts. Whatever the reason, there is not the joy, love, and peace that we might expect in such a land.

You can pray for Western Samoa

1 Lord Jesus, please help the churches in Western Samoa to teach families how truly to live God's way.

2 Help young people attracted by a Western way of life to realize that true happiness is only found in you.

3 Use the daily Christian radio broadcasts to bring Samoans to new life in you.

4 May many more Samoans come to know you, and be willing to take your love and truth to other lands.

5 When old Samoan customs are linked with evil spirits, help Christians to refuse to take part, and to speak out against them.

6 Help church leaders in Western Samoa to love Jesus with all their hearts.

7 May the message of the Bible, read so often by Samoans, also be understood and obeyed in their lives.

WOLOF

OFFICIALS AND TRADESMEN OF THE SENEGAL RIVER VALLEY

Night watchman

Modou, a frightened old Wolof man decorated with charms, cautiously opened the big gates and entered the garden of the missionaries' home in north Senegal. He was applying for a job as a night watchman, but didn't know what to expect from the foreign ladies who lived there and who were said to be Christians. He badly needed work, or he would never have come.

Barbara, one of the lady missionaries, had been alone in the house one night when burglars came. As they ripped the bars off the windows at the back of the house, Barbara fled through the front door and locked herself in the garage. She could hear them hunting through her house and prayed desperately that they wouldn't break into the garage. God heard her prayers. It was after this fright that she decided she needed a night watchman.

Old Modou took the job. He soon lost his fear of Barbara and her friend Jenny and came to respect them. Unlike some white women he had seen, they dressed more like Wolof women and were careful not to be out on the streets after dark.

W for Wolofs – strong Muslims and proud, Their tall white-robed figures stand out in a crowd.

Motorbike missionaries

He noticed that Barbara and Jenny were thoughtful and kind. They visited sick people, traveling many miles by motorbike to hold clinics in the villages. Even the frequent wind storms which filled their home with dust and dirt could not stop them from being cheerful. Above all, Modou saw that they loved their God and every day read God's book and prayed to him.

Soon Modou thought of Barbara and Jenny as if they were his own daughters. He gladly listened to a tape of the Bible in the Wolof language which they gave him. He could hardly believe his ears. How marvelous and holy the Christian God seemed! At times he liked what he heard so much that he clapped his hands with amazement. He listened to eight chapters of the book of Romans and then begged to take the tape home to play to his family.

M. Filidis

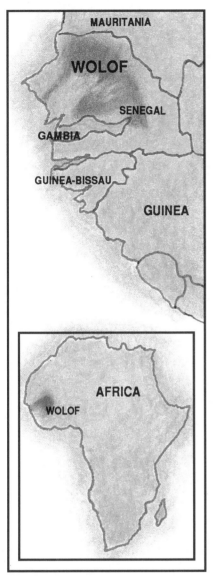

Because he works as a servant, Modou is looked down on by other Wolof people. He is afraid of what his friends, sons, and sons-in-law would say and do if he were to believe in Jesus. What would the *Marabouts* (Muslim leaders) say? They have much power in Richard Toll, the oddly-named town where Modou lives. Several other Muslims also want to follow Jesus but are afraid.

You can pray for the Wolof

The Wolof are a proud people. Many hold top positions in business and government in Senegal. Although strong Muslims, they still use charms and consult spirits. The New Testament, some hymns, and Christian books have been translated into Wolof. Several missionaries are working among them, but as yet there are only about fifteen Wolof Christians in the whole of Senegal, out of a total of two million.

1 Dear Lord, please send more Christian workers to the Wolof people.

2 Bring Wolof children and their parents together to listen to your Word and accept your love and forgiveness.

3 Help Wolof men like Modou, who have heard your message, to leave Islam and animism and turn to Jesus with all their hearts.

4 Help missionaries speak the Wolof language and show the love and purity of Jesus in their lives.

5 Break the power of evil spirits in the lives of the Wolof people. Help them to know that nothing is stronger than your power.

6 Keep missionaries safe and free from fear. Help them to show how wonderful and loving you are.

7 Bring together some Wolof Christians to start the first Wolof church.

XINJIANG

LAND OF WINDSWEPT DESERTS

The Xinjiang region in the far west of China is mostly windswept desert, with some high mountains, and much mineral wealth. Many of the people who live here are nomads. It is a harsh place to live – sometimes extremely hot, sometimes extremely cold. The government has moved many people to Xinjiang from other parts of China to try to control the Muslim peoples who make up more than half of its population.

The Uighur are the most numerous of these different people groups. They live in oases on the slopes of the Celestial Mountains around the cruel Takla Makan ("You will never come out") Desert. Uighurs live in flat-roofed, five-roomed houses made of sun-baked mud bricks. They grow grapes, melons, wheat, cotton, cabbages, and sunflowers.

Although the Chinese Communist government once tried to get rid of all religions, Muslims remained faithful to their beliefs, still praying five times a day. Recently the government has changed its attitude and has given money to help rebuild mosques; thousands of Muslim books have been given out and an Islamic college has opened.

Christianity has not done so well. Several thousand people are Christians, but these are mostly from a Chinese background. There are hardly any Christians among the Muslim people groups like the Uighurs. Missionaries cannot go there, but Christians can work there in jobs like teaching English.

XINJIANG

the huge region in China's far west, Where the land is harsh and the wind takes no rest.

An angry father

Life is difficult for many young people in Xinjiang. Azaz, a teacher, hadn't seen his best pupil, Ayshangal, for days. He stooped to enter a small restaurant beside the bazaar.

"Come in, sir, our food is ready." To his surprise it was Ayshangal who was offering to serve him. As she saw her teacher she looked embarrassed.

"Hey! Ayshangal . . ." began Azaz. A man lay sprawled on a bed staring angrily, so Azaz said nothing. The man shouted at Ayshangal, "Don't stand there staring! Give the customer a cup of tea."

Ayshangal hurried to the fire. Azaz looked around. The ceiling and walls were stained and dusty with spiderwebs. A money box beside him, the man stuffed tobacco into his pipe. "Are you Ayshangal's father?" Azaz asked. "I'm her teacher."

The man raised himself from the bed. "Ugh! She's not going to school any more. I never went and I'm making good money." He opened the box and displayed a wad of 100 yuan notes.

"Ayshangal is still young," stammered Azaz. "She should go to school. She's clever."

"She doesn't want to go to school any more," her father said, puffing on his pipe.

Ayshangal appeared with a plate of noodles. Her face showed she disagreed. "Do you want to go to school or not?" Azaz asked her. Ayshangal stared at the ground, then looked at her teacher with a flash of hope. "I would love to study but . . ." Whack!

Ayshangal's soft face showed the print of her father's hand. Azaz caught his arm as he went to strike her again, begging him to let Ayshangal continue school.

It was useless. As he left he heard the girl crying, "Father, I want to go to school. Can't I please finish school?"

You can pray for Xinjiang

1 Lord Jesus, please help children and young people like Ayshangal to turn to you in their troubles, and send Christians to be their friends.

2 May Chinese believers in Xinjiang want to tell Muslims about your love.

3 Send people to produce Christian books in the languages of the Uighurs, Kazakhs, Kirghiz, and other Muslim peoples who live in Xinjiang.

4 Send Christians to work among these Muslim people groups, to learn their languages and explain to them who Jesus is and what he has done for them.

5 Help Muslims who become Christians to tell others how great you are and how much you love them.

6 Break the power of Islam over people's lives, by the power of your Holy Spirit.

7 Help people making Christian radio programs in Uighur and other languages. May people hear and understand your message.

XHOSA

RED-BLANKET PEOPLE OF THE TRANSKEI

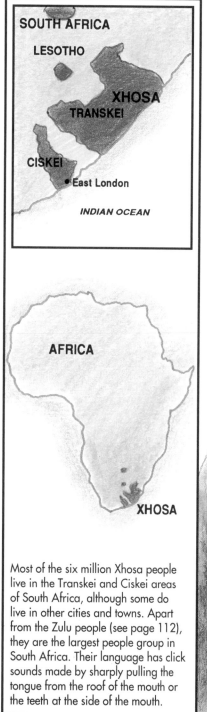

SOUTH AFRICA

LESOTHO

XHOSA
TRANSKEI

CISKEI
●East London

INDIAN OCEAN

AFRICA

XHOSA

Most of the six million Xhosa people live in the Transkei and Ciskei areas of South Africa, although some do live in other cities and towns. Apart from the Zulu people (see page 112), they are the largest people group in South Africa. Their language has click sounds made by sharply pulling the tongue from the roof of the mouth or the teeth at the side of the mouth.

When I lived in South Africa, I met many Xhosa children. Zawa and Sikhono, two boys from a big family in Johannesburg, became Christians and were invited to a children's camp. It was great fun, and they talked nonstop about it when they returned home. Their drunkard father and overworked mother were astonished by all Zawa and Sikhono told them.

Some months later we showed a film of the camp in their school courtyard. When it was over their father jumped up to say he'd started going to church and was so happy that he'd forgotten to drink beer and now gave his wife enough money to care for the family! His wife then got up and said Jesus had changed her sons and husband so much that she too had become a Christian.

X is for Xhosa, who speak with a click; Their tongues and their teeth perform quite a trick!

Angry with Satan!

Daniel, a Xhosa boy who lives in the city of Pretoria, became a Christian in a meeting in a big tent. One day I met him looking very grumpy. "What's the matter?" I asked.

"I am very angry with Satan. I was in a shop just now and he told me to steal like I used to."

"Did you?" I asked.

"No, but what nerve he's got bothering me like that," he replied. He already realized who his enemy was and how to deal with him.

Free rides

Bhekinkosi was one of the naughtiest boys in Gugulethu, a poor part of Cape Town. He would jump on the back of moving vans for free rides, but as he was crippled in one leg and couldn't run very fast, he was often caught and beaten by angry drivers. However, he was not trying to be naughty when he went to a Christian meeting. Bhekinkosi was very serious. With tears rolling down his face he prayed, "Lord Jesus, it is I, Bhekinkosi. I'm a bad boy. Please make my heart clean and come and live in me forever."

Village life

These boys all come from the towns, but life is quite different in Xhosa villages. Families live in beautifully rounded huts with a fireplace in the center and mud benches built against the walls. Village children work hard, walking miles to fetch water, firewood, and food, and small boys control big herds of cattle with great skill. Village women wear black turbans and red blankets which they dye themselves, but Christians wear Western clothes, because red blankets are worn when worshiping evil spirits.

The Xhosa people love to sing in lovely harmony and even simple village schools have well-trained choirs. I will always remember dancing and singing with some Xhosa Christians on the mountainside at night. They sang, "This Jesus of mine, he has power." Let's pray that this power of God will work in the lives of many Xhosa people.

You can pray for the Xhosa

1 Dear Lord, set the Xhosa people free by your power, from witchcraft and ancestor worship.

2 Help Xhosa Christians to write Bible songs and choruses in the Xhosa language for their own people.

3 Send Christians to teach Xhosa children the Word of God.

4 Send Christian leaders to run Bible camps and Sunday schools for Xhosa children.

5 Send Christians with your love and truth to all the scattered villages of the Transkei and Ciskei.

6 Help politicians in South Africa to turn away from all they have done wrong, and have faith in you.

7 May Xhosa Christians help others to be happy, both white and black, in the troubled land of South Africa.

YEMEN

LAND OF THE QUEEN OF SHEBA

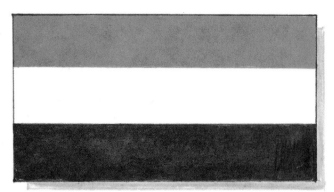

Do you remember the Bible story of the Queen of Sheba? You can read about how she and King Solomon gave each other amazingly expensive gifts in 1 Kings 10:1–13.

Her kingdom was in what is now the Arabian land of Yemen, and the great cities of her day are buried beneath the desert sands. Over 1,500 years after the Queen of Sheba lived, Yemen became Muslim. For many years it was thought to be one of the most mysterious countries in the world, since it was almost completely cut off from outsiders. Yemen is a beautiful land, with high mountain peaks and lovely six and seven-story houses made of mud and wonderfully decorated.

Guests to dinner

In his white turban and *zanna* (ankle-length cotton tunic) Gadeed watched closely as his father greeted his guests. Europeans had never visited them before. Everything interested them: the mud-walled pen where the few goats were tethered, the room storing grain from the harvest, even his sister making bread.

Gadeed, too, watched as his sister kneaded the dough and slapped it expertly against the sides of the mud oven. A fire blazed at the bottom, and, unless she was very careful, the flat bread would slip off the side into the fire. Later, sitting together on the floor, the men ate

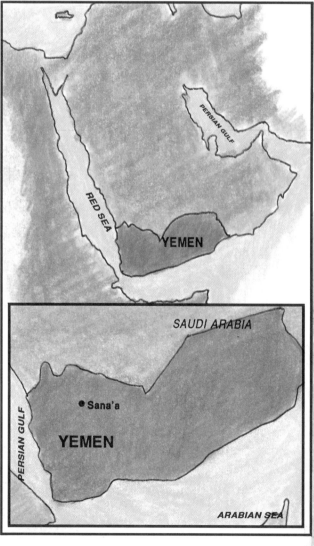

chicken, rice, and vegetables. Gadeed carefully poured the coffee. Soon his father would show the guests his new water pump and vineyard.

First, however, he solemnly placed a copy of the Koran on a special wooden stand and eagerly read aloud several passages about Isa (which is the Muslim name for Jesus).

Y

stands for Yemen, with daggers and veils, Spices and grapes and Arabian tales.

He seemed excited to find so many places where Jesus was mentioned and to read such wonderful things about him. Gadeed was sorry when the Koran was put away and the guests talked of other things: silk and gold carpets in the *souk* (market), decorated glass windows, and curved daggers.

Suddenly a booming noise from the nearby mosque made the guests jump. Through a loudspeaker a voice was calling people to prayer. The guests longed to tell the veiled women and the fierce-looking men that Jesus really is the Son of God, who offers them complete forgiveness and a new life.

North and South

For many years North and South Yemen were two separate countries. South Yemen was Communist, while North Yemen, made up of warring tribes who lived by trading and bargaining, was strongly Muslim. Then in 1990 the two countries became one, with Sana'a as its capital. The new president has a difficult job in uniting his fourteen million people. For example, women in the South do not want to wear a veil like the ladies of the North, while the Northerners are determined to keep their religious way of life.

For a long time Christians have tried to talk about Jesus in Yemen. This has been difficult because Muslims are proud of their religion, believing

Christianity is only for slaves and conquered people. All Yemenis are expected to be Muslims. Families are very close, and for one member of the family to choose another religion is unthinkable. Sadly, too, Muslims think all Westerners are Christians, so the poor behavior of some soldiers, politicians, and tourists makes them think that Christianity is bad.

You can pray for Yemen

1 Lord Jesus, please use Arabic Bibles to help Muslims in Yemen understand that you alone are the way to God.

2 Make it easy for Christian radio broadcasts to be heard in Yemen.

3 Help Christians in the West to invite their Muslim neighbors into their homes and show them your love.

4 Help Muslims reading the Koran to notice what it says about you and to want to know more.

5 Please speak to Muslims in Yemen in dreams and visions, showing them your truth.

6 Please make more jobs available in Yemen, especially in hospitals and schools, for Christians from overseas.

7 May many Yemeni boys and girls like Gadeed have the opportunity to believe in you.

YAO

CHILDREN OF THE DRAGON-DOG

Fay Foo lived in the village of River Mountain in north Thailand. For the last few weeks the village had buzzed with excitement. Even daily work in the rice and opium fields was neglected. Thai officials were asking those who wanted to live in America to go to the refugee center nearby.

Y for the Yao, whose old habits and ways
Are having to change as they face modern days.

The invitation was meant for refugees from the neighboring country of Laos, but it seemed any Yao wishing to go was accepted by the officials. Some lied, saying they were refugees in order to get to America. Fay Foo's family were Christians and had lived all their lives in Thailand. They felt that they must tell the truth, even if it meant the end of their dreams of a new life in the USA.

The Yao listened eagerly to cassettes telling of the wonderful life in America – supermarkets, cars, televisions, nice houses, and plenty of jobs. Most of the villagers would give anything to get there.

After more than eighty families had left, the village seemed almost empty. When her best friend went, Fay Foo and her brother begged their parents to put their names down too.

YAO

SOUTH EAST ASIA

CHINA

VIETNAM

MYANMAR (BURMA)

YAO

LAOS

THAILAND

The name "Children of the Dragon-dog" comes from a Yao legend about a "dragon-dog" who killed the enemy of the Emperor of China. He claimed the emperor's daughter as his wife. They had six sons and six daughters and the story says that the Yao people are descended from these twelve.

There are three million Yao, living in places as far apart as China, Vietnam, Laos, France and America. This makes it difficult to reach them and tell them the good news about Jesus. Thirty thousand live in Thailand, like Fay Foo and her family, and only a small number of these are Christians.

Couldn't they tell just one little lie to get to that marvelous new land?

The Jesus way

Fay Foo's father explained gently, "When we followed the spirits, we thought the most important things in life were money, our fields, and our feasts; but now we know better. We have found that the Jesus way is wonderful. At first we left the spirits and did Christian things, but it was only a change on the outside. Later we realized that Jesus wanted a change deep inside our hearts. Now we know our sins are forgiven and we have peace, even when we're sad and have problems. Jesus has promised us a home in heaven which is a thousand times more wonderful than America. We're not going to make the Lord Jesus sad by telling lies."

Fay Foo thought about her father's words. She'd noticed the difference between the Christians and animists in River Mountain. Many Christians could read and were respected because they gave helpful advice and prayed with sick people. They would even pray for sick pigs, if their owners were afraid these valuable animal might die. They no longer grew opium, although it brought in more money than any other crop, because they knew that those who smoke it become poor and miserable.

Yes, even if it meant staying in River Mountain while her friends went to America, Fay Foo was glad her family was following the Jesus way.

You can pray for the Yao

1 Dear Lord, please help many Yao to realize that they need you to change them from the inside so that they can be free from the power of evil spirits.

2 Teach Yao Christians to give money to support pastors and evangelists to take your message to other Yao villages.

3 Help Yao Christians to be honest even when they are tempted to tell lies to get what they want.

4 Fill pastors and evangelists with your joy and peace so they may not give up serving you to make money.

5 Help Yao children from Christian families to trust Jesus for themselves.

6 Help Christians here, in America, to tell the Yao people living near them about you.

7 Help Yao Christians to love the New Testament and to learn verses by heart.

ZIMBABWE

BETWEEN THE ZAMBEZI AND THE LIMPOPO

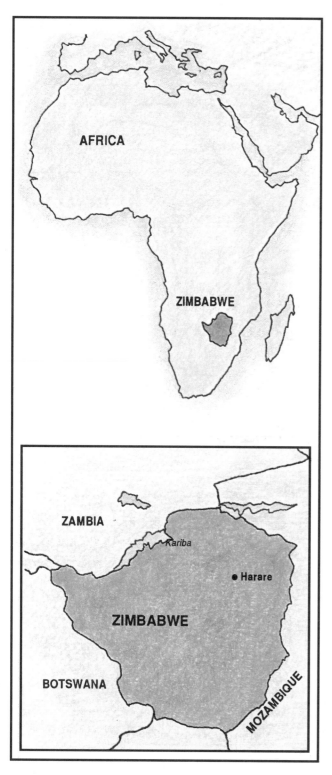

AFRICA

ZIMBABWE

ZAMBIA

Kariba

● Harare

ZIMBABWE

BOTSWANA

MOZAMBIQUE

Zimbabwe is a very beautiful country. The Victoria Falls on the Zambezi River plunge into a deep, narrow gorge. The falling water makes so much spray that the area around is like a rain forest. The local name, "the smoke that thunders," describes its cloud of spray and its roaring water.

Kariba, one of the world's largest man-made lakes, stretches for 160 miles through spectacular countryside. Elephant herds, lions, cheetahs, hyenas, and rhino can still be seen in the national parks. Plenty of food is grown, but some people are still hungry – such as the one and a half million unemployed, many poor farmers, and thousands of refugees from the war in nearby Mozambique.

Two main tribes
Seven out of ten people are from the MaShona tribe, and about two out of ten are MaNdebele. Many years ago the MaNdebele conquered the MaShona and some bad feeling still exists between them. White people ruled the country until 1980, when they lost power. Less than one percent of the population is white. People from the different races need to learn to be true friends and proud of their new country.

Kicking the stove

Stephen Lungu couldn't believe his ears. The preacher in the mission tent seemed to be talking clearly about him. "Some people are so mixed up inside they even kick paraffin stoves," he said.

Stephen and his friends had come to the Christian meeting to make trouble. Now he suddenly remembered how that morning his paraffin stove had refused to light. He was furious because it meant he would have to go to work without a cup of tea.

In his anger he kicked the stove across the floor, just as the preacher had said!

God was speaking to Stephen in a surprising way, and he suddenly knew that he had to ask Jesus to forgive his sins and change his heart. So he knelt right down there in the tent and asked Jesus to be Lord of his life.

Stephen knew that one thing he needed to do immediately was to forgive his mother. He had hated her for many years because when he was small she had left him and his little sister to hunt through dustbins for their

food. As he grew up he had even planned to kill her if he ever met her again. But God gave him the power to forgive, and eventually he even helped his mother to put her trust in Jesus.

Going abroad

Many Zimbabweans have become strong Christians through the work among young people of missions like Scripture Union. Some work fearlessly in Zimbabwe, others have moved to other countries. Saluh Daka went as a missionary to Mozambique, where he was put in prison for his faith; he is now a missionary in Cameroon. Oliver Ntambo is a mission leader in England, and Newman Mzvondiwa is a missionary in Japan.

Sadly, many Christians are still afraid of evil spirits and return to animism when troubles come. African Christian leaders say that almost everyone in Zimbabwe is under the control of tribal chiefs, and these chiefs are chosen by spirit rituals. The whole country needs to be set free from the power of the spirit world.

Z

for Zimbabwe, with elephant herds, Crocodiles, rhinos, and beautiful birds.

You can pray for Zimbabwe

1 Lord Jesus, please give evangelists from different missions the power to bring young people to faith in you.

2 May missions, churches, and youth groups teach Christians your Word so they can understand it better.

3 Give Christians courage to burn their charms and refuse to take part in spirit worship.

4 Help Christians to care for and give to the poor, the unemployed, and the refugees in their country.

5 Please send missionaries from Zimbabwe to other lands, especially nearby Mozambique which is so needy.

6 May people see you at work in the lives of Saluh, Oliver, Newman, and other missionaries from Zimbabwe.

7 Thank you that Christians from all races can feel they belong to one family. May this love for one another grow in Zimbabwe.

111

ZULUS

MIGHTY WARRIORS OF SOUTHERN AFRICA

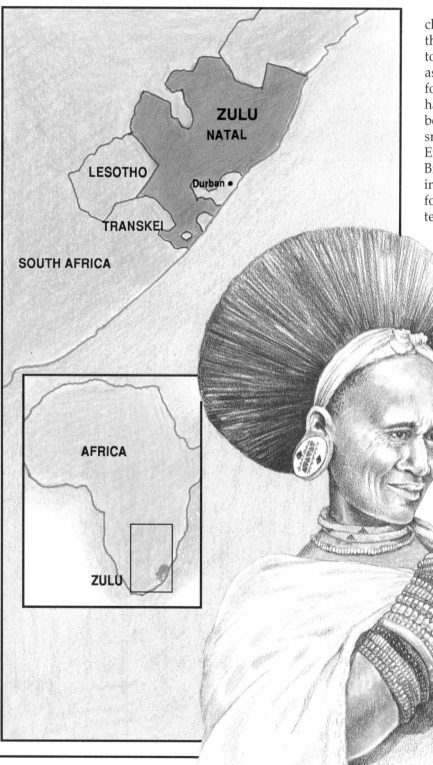

A brave singer

It was cold in our mission tent in Natal, South Africa. Thandiwe, a young Zulu girl, was wearing her father's jacket, the sleeves turned back and the hem a few inches from her ankles. This did not stop her from singing bravely into the microphone to start the meeting, and her small face was shining with happiness.

As I sat surrounded by dusty children singing loudly, I knew that I was where God wanted me to be. He had called me to Africa as a missionary when I was only four years old. My godmother had given me a children's prayer book. On the cover were three small children going to church: an English boy, a girl carrying a Bible, and an African boy dressed in a striped blanket. I knew then for certain that God wanted me to tell African children about Jesus. Through that tent mission in Klaarwater Township God did some wonderful things among the Zulu children. Before long over thirty children loved Jesus so much that they started preaching in our tent and nearby.

Z is for Zulus, whose regiments brave Swept over the land in a conquering wave!

Chicken's blood

Beaumont was about to steal from a local store when he noticed the tent. He came in and became a Christian. For four years Beaumont preached about Jesus outside shops, on buses, and while visiting people in their homes. Then some thugs became jealous of his fame as a preacher, and one day they beat him up and he died, a martyr for Jesus.

Mrs. Kadebe, who lived near the tent, was sacrificing a chicken to God when I visited her. "I am a Christian," she said. But I told her, "No one who understands the sacrifice of Jesus would offer a chicken's blood to God."

Mrs. Kadebe couldn't sleep for nights until she finally understood that Jesus died so she could be forgiven and freed from the fear of evil spirits. She became a powerful evangelist and traveled to many nearby towns and villages preaching God's Word.

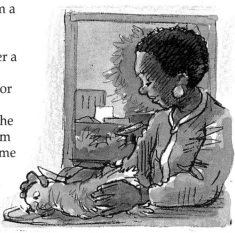

Zulu warriors

The seven million Zulus are known for their great *impis*, armies of well-disciplined highly-trained men. They are the only African army to have defeated the British in battle. They still have a king and a royal family, but the glory of their past is now only a memory. When the men went to work in the mines and cities of South Africa, their way of life changed and their once great feasts and ceremonies stopped.

Many Zulus call themselves Christians but few have given up ancestor worship and witchcraft. Sadly some churches mix up the Christian message with practices and teachings that relate to spirit worship. So new Zulu *impis* are needed, *impis* for Jesus!

You can pray for the Zulus

1 Lord Jesus, may Zulu Christians become leaders in their own churches. Help them to make Christian young people a mighty *impi* for you.

2 May Christian camps help children to know you and learn how to live in a way that pleases you.

3 Give Christians wisdom to help the many young Zulus who have no education and no jobs.

4 Help Christians of all races in South Africa to love, respect, and care for one another.

5 Give your Holy Spirit to Chief Buthelezi, one of the most important Zulu leaders, and help him to lead his people in your way.

6 Help people realize that you can set them free from the fear and evil of Zulu witch doctors.

7 Please help everyone who is telling the good news about Jesus to the Zulu people. May people hear you speaking to them today through your Word, the Bible.

ANIMISM AND ANCESTOR WORSHIP

Animists believe that there are spirits living in everything; in stones, trees, seeds, water, and in people, dead or alive. They believe these spirits can cause bad things to happen such as quarrels, sickness, and drought.

Sacrifices

To try to stop the spirits causing harm, or to get something from them that they want, animists offer sacrifices to the spirits. They may sacrifice a chicken to get good crops, or tie some hair to a palm tree to get many coconuts. Some wear special bracelets or charms (called fetishes) which they think have magical powers to protect them from harm.

Animism is found all over the world, especially in countries where there is no other main religion. Animist beliefs are also mixed into some types of Hinduism, Buddhism, and Islam, and even in Christian churches where believers have not learned enough about what the Bible teaches.

Witchcraft

There are men and women with special knowledge of the spirit world called witch-doctors, shamans, or sorcerers. Some people go to them for help and protection from spirits and witchcraft, but usually this does more harm than good. Some people ask for "medicine" to hurt others.

Full of fear

Most animists are full of fear. They may fear places, trees, rivers, strangers, the way somebody looks at them, or just simple objects like money or a knife that they find near their home. If the Akha people in Thailand see a loris, a small kind of monkey, in the forest, they are frightened to use the fields they have prepared for sowing. They must sacrifice a pig to the spirits and have to work on another farmer's land to earn a living until they can prepare a new field for themselves.

It is not easy for an animist to leave these beliefs, but Christians who know that Jesus is more powerful than evil spirits will have the courage to do so. They will burn their charms, fetishes, and everything they used to believe in, and at last be free from the fear and misery of animism.

Ancestor worship

Many animists also worship their ancestors, family members from earlier generations who are now dead. They believe that people who die become spirits and are able to both help and harm those who are still alive. So they sacrifice to these spirits, hoping that they will help them grow good crops or have more money or children. They believe the spirits of their ancestors can cure sickness or other problems in the family. If they forget to worship or sacrifice to their ancestors and things go wrong they believe that they are being punished for neglecting them.

But even when animists sacrifice and worship in this way, troubles still come. So they believe someone else in the family must have sinned and made the ancestors angry. As you can imagine, this makes people very suspicious and does not help to make happy families.

BUDDHISM

Prince Gautama lived in India about 2,500 years ago. His parents wanted him to be happy, so as he grew up they kept him from seeing anything that might make him sad. However, one day when riding in his chariot he saw first a beggar covered in sores, then a feeble old man, and finally someone who had died.

Many lives
It made Gautama unhappy to realize that people get old and sick and die. He had been taught that when we die we start another life, or are reborn as a different person, or even as an animal or insect. This belief is called "reincarnation." He knew nothing about the God who loves and cares for us all through our lives.

Thinking deeply
Gautama wondered how a person could stop being reborn again and again. He thought deeply for so long that his mind became blank.

He wanted nothing for himself; he just wanted to help other people and never to hurt any living creature. He felt that if he could stay like that, when he died he would not be reborn. He did not believe in heaven, he simply thought that he would become nothing, and he taught many others these beliefs too.

The Buddha
Gautama's followers call him the Buddha, the "enlightened one." Although he did not believe in God, and did not wish to be worshiped, many people who follow his teachings worship and pray to him as if he were a god. They are called Buddhists.

Buddhists believe that by meditating – sitting still and thinking deeply – they will become better people, so that they too can stop being reborn. But they don't believe anyone except Gautama has ever achieved this. Most people, of course, are too busy to sit still all day meditating!

Monks
Some Buddhists live in monasteries for a few weeks while others spend their entire lives as monks. Even monks can't sit meditating all day. They go begging with a little bowl, hoping that some kind person will fill it with rice and perhaps a hot pepper or tasty vegetable. They live simply, have shaved heads and bare feet, and wear yellow robes.

What the Bible says
The Bible tells us that however hard we try, we cannot be really good people without Jesus in our lives. We only live once on this earth and if we are sorry for the wrong things we do, and ask the Lord Jesus to forgive us, we shall live with him one day in heaven.

Buddhists need to know the truth about God and his Son Jesus. Jesus is the only way to heaven, where God the Father lives with those who love him. In heaven there will be no more of the sorrow, sickness, and death that made Gautama sad.

HINDUISM

Hinduism began about 3,500 years ago in India. There are thousands of gods in Hinduism, but only a few of them are actually worshiped. Hindus believe Brahman is the greatest, but he doesn't do anything.

Castes

Every Hindu is born into a group called a caste. Some castes are thought to be higher and purer than others. At the top is the priestly caste, next come rulers and soldiers, then traders and shopkeepers. Lower caste people sweep, wash clothes, repair shoes, and generally are the servants of the higher castes.

Life after life

Hindus believe in reincarnation, that is, that when people die they come back to life again as animals or people. Hindus also believe in something called *karma.. Karma* means that the way people behaved in their past life affects their place in this life, and what they do in this life will decide their place in the next.

If people keep the rules of their caste they believe that they will be reborn into a higher caste. They believe that eventually they will stop living as people, but become part of the god Brahman. The rebirths may go on for ever and ever as Hindus can never be sure they have done everything correctly.

Holy places

Hindus make pilgrimages to holy places like Varanasi on the River Ganges in India. They believe bathing in the river will purify them from sins such as not keeping their caste rules or touching things they believe are unclean. Sin for a Hindu has little to do with breaking God's commands or hurting other people.

Hindus have altars in their homes and in temples where they worship brightly-painted gods and goddesses, offering food, money, and prayers, hoping to find peace and freedom from evil spirits.

Sacred cows

Most Hindus are vegetarians. They believe animals and insects have souls, so they won't eat meat or take life if they can avoid it. Cows are thought to be especially sacred, so they are allowed to wander freely in the streets, eating whatever they like even when people are starving nearby.

There are over 700 million Hindus in the world, mostly in India. Some people believe that through yoga, meditation and the New Age movement, Hinduism is spreading to the West. It is true many people in so-called "Christian" countries are taking a great interest in some Hindu beliefs.

Pandita Ramabai

When Ramabai was a little girl, her father taught her the Hindu scriptures in Sanskrit, a very old religious language. Many Hindus were angry because their holy books say women, whether high or low caste, are evil, worse even than demons. They say a woman's only god is her husband, so he may treat her as he wishes. But some Hindu teachers, amazed at Ramabai's knowledge of their holy books, called her Pandita, a special Hindu title no other woman has ever been given!

Amazed by the gospel

Ramabai's parents and brother died of starvation and sickness in spite of all their obedience to the Hindu religion, and so she lost her faith in Hinduism. One day Ramabai read Luke's Gospel and was amazed to find it so real and true. Several years later she became a Christian.

Ramabai had kept all the Hindu rules and found only sorrow. As a Christian she found joy and peace. She opened many orphanages, hospitals, and schools, and started industries where disabled and blind people could earn a living. Ramabai experienced both Hinduism and Christianity in her life, and proved that Jesus Christ is the one true God.

ISLAM

Muslims follow the religion called Islam. This was founded by the prophet Muhammad, who was born 1,400 years ago in Mecca, Saudi Arabia. He believed the angel Gabriel gave him messages from God. These messages were put together into the Muslim holy book called the Koran.

Muhammad became an orphan at the age of six and was cared for by his uncle. The Koran tells the story of Muhammad as a child being visited by two angels. They opened his chest and removed an impure blood clot from his heart and then closed up his chest again. Muslims believe this means Muhammad was purified and shown to be a prophet from his childhood.

Waiting for judgment
Muhammad asked several times for forgiveness for his sins and believed he was a sinner. The Koran teaches that when Muhammad died he did not go to heaven but is still waiting for the day of judgment. Whenever Muslims say Muhammad's name they must pray for him to receive peace. This means Muslims are not sure that Muhammad is forgiven by God and so they can't be certain that they are forgiven either. Muslims are therefore very afraid as they wait for judgment.

Muhammad taught that there is only one God, Allah, so Muslims think it is very wrong for Christians to believe in God the Father, God the Son, and God the Holy Spirit as one God.

Five Pillars
There are five duties each good Muslim must perform, called the "Five Pillars of Islam." These are:

1. Declaring their faith by repeating, "There is no God but Allah, and Muhammad is his prophet."
2. Saying prayers five times a day – before sunrise, after midday, mid-afternoon, after sunset, and after nightfall – while facing towards the city of Mecca.
3. Giving alms of money or goods to poor people.
4. Fasting during Ramadan, the ninth month in the Islamic calendar. During Ramadan food and drink may be taken only between sunset and sunrise.
5. Making the *Hajj*, a pilgrimage to Mecca in the twelfth month of the Islamic calendar. All Muslims are expected to go on the *Hajj* once in their lifetime.

Mosques
The building in which Muslims worship is called a mosque. Mosques usually have a tall tower called a minaret from the top of which the call to prayer goes out five times a day.

Divided
Just as Muslims believe that Allah is one, so they believe in one Islamic people, and that all Muslims should be united. However there are still major divisions in Islam, the largest being between the Sunni and the Shi'a Muslims, and this is a great problem to them.

Muslims are usually more modest in their clothing than Westerners. A religious Muslim would never wear shorts or tight clothes. Muslim women often wear trousers covered by a skirt, a long-sleeved top or dress, and keep their heads covered.

Men and women
Muslim men are thought to be superior to women and worth twice as much, and children are taught this. The Koran encourages men to beat their wives if they anger them, and men may have up to four wives. The way women are treated varies from one Muslim country to another.

When we speak to Muslims it isn't kind to speak of Muhammad's failures or the things we don't like about Islam. It is better to tell them of the love and holiness of Jesus, his wonderful words and deeds, and how we can be close to God through him. Muslims do have a respect for the Bible and are often willing to read the stories about Jesus in the New Testament, which they call the Injil.

WORD LIST

Animism: the belief that all objects and living things have souls.

Antidote: a cure or remedy for a poison.

Arthritis: a disease that makes one or more of the joints painful and stiff.

Bazaar: an Oriental (Eastern) marketplace.

Blasphemy: speaking or acting in scornful disrespect for God.

Betel nut: the seed of the betel palm, chewed as a mild drug. It makes the teeth turn red.

Bush: woodland or untilled district.

Christian: a person who says he believes in Christ.

Civil War: war between parties, people groups, or inhabitants with different interests within the same nation.

Clan: part of a tribe usually having the same family name.

Cobra: a poisonous snake of Africa and India.

Communist: a supporter of communism. Communism is a form of government in which the state controls everything.

Compound: an enclosure or village where people live.

Conflict: a struggle or clash.

Coptic: the ancient Christian Church of Egypt and Ethiopia.

Coup: a sudden violent or illegal take over of a government. (From the French– *coup d'etat*.)

Culture: the customs and values of a people.

Correspondence course: lessons sent through the mail.

Dictator: a tyrant who rules with unlimited power.

Dowry: the money or property brought by a woman to her husband at marriage.

Enforced: made sure the law was obeyed.

Enlightened: having spiritual or religious understanding.

Epilepsy: a sickness which causes a fit or spasm.

Evangelical: one who believes personal commitment and faith in Christ as Savior to be necessary for salvation, and that the whole Bible is God's Word.

Evangelist: one who preaches the gospel to those who have not yet believed as above.

Extremists: people who approve of, or behave in, a biased way and don't see any value in other opinions.

Fable: a short, moral story usually with animals as characters.

Fasted: went without food to spend time praying to God.

Guerilla: a member of an irregular armed force fighting against the army or police of a country.

Heretic: a person rejected for holding beliefs contrary to the accepted teachings of his or her church.

Home-rule: within their own area a group may rule themselves.

Icon: a religious picture of Christ, the Virgin Mary, or a saint.

Idol: an image of a god used in worship.

Initiation: a ceremony, often secret, in which new members are accepted into a group.

Irrigation: the supplying of water by artificial means, where there is not enough rain to grow crops.

Islam: the religion of Muslims.

Islamic: adjective – see Islam.

Koran: sacred book of Islam.

Lama: a priest or monk of Tibetan Buddhism.

Lamaseries: monasteries of Buddhist lamas or priests.

Latin (*as in Latin America*): all countries of the Americas where Spanish or Portuguese is the official language. These came from Latin, the language of the ancient Romans.

Leprosy: a skin disease that damages the nerves and cripples people.

Loris: a small slender, climbing lemur, active at night.

Lutheran: a follower of Martin Luther, or a member of a Lutheran church.

Martin Luther: German leader of the churches of the West, called Protestant, which separated from the Roman Catholic Church in the sixteenth century.

Meditation: sitting quietly, thinking deeply about religious matters.

Messiah: the king the Jews are expecting (Jesus).

Migraine: A bad headache, sometimes causing a person to be sick and their sight to go fuzzy.

Mosque: a Muslim place of worship.

Muslim: a follower of the religion of Islam.

New Age Movement: a modern mixture of many religions, offering peace, light, and love.

Nomad: a member of a people or tribe who move from place to place to find pasture and food.

Oasis: a fertile part of the desert where there is water.

Opium: a drug made from poppy seeds. Some people depend on it and it makes them ill.

Orthodox: ancient form of Christianity still practiced today.

Parsees: people who follow a very old religion, Zoroastrianism, that came from Iran before Islam.

Peninsula: a narrow strip of land reaching out into the sea.

Pidgin: a language made up of some parts of two or more languages.

Plateau: a wide, mainly flat, area of high land.

Prostrating: lying face downwards in submission.

Ration book: a book of tickets allowing people to buy a fixed amount of food and provisions in time of war or when they are scarce.

Revival: a reawakening of the church to faith, new love, and service of God.

Rituals: the formal acts that take place in ceremonies.

Romany: another name for Gypsy and the Gypsy language.

Script: a style of writing, or an alphabet.

Serf: a person bound to the land and its owner. He or she is not free to move away.

Shamans: priests of shamanism who believe the world is filled with good and evil spirits.

Sharia: the laws and teachings of Islam to be obeyed by all Muslims.

Shintoism: a religion of Japan in which several gods are worshiped, the chief of which is believed to be the ancestor of the emperor.

Sikhs: members of a movement that sprang from Hinduism in the 16th century who believe in one god. Sikhs do not cut their hair and adult men wear turbans.

Sin: disobeying God's will as shown in his Word.

Sorcerers: wizards or magicians – people who seek to control and use magic powers.

Taboo: something that is forbidden, or not approved of, for religious reasons.

Termite: an ant-like insect found in warm climates, a destructive eater of wood and paper.

Theocracy: government by a god, goddess, or priesthood.

Thug: a tough and violent man.

Township: a planned town where people live while working in a nearby city.

Venom: a poison, usually coming from the bite or sting of certain snakes or scorpions.

Voodoo: a religious system which came from Africa in which witchcraft and contact with spirits is practiced.

Witch-doctor: a person possessing magical powers who may use these to heal or harm people.

Yoga: Hindu physical and mental exercises which aim to contact the supreme being.

Zoroastrian: a believer in the religion begun in Iran by Zoroaster.

WHAT CAN I DO NOW?

There are so many things children can do to be involved in missions right now. Here are a few ideas to help you get started:

1. Have you found one of the people groups in this book particularly interesting? Why not adopt that people group and find out all you can about them and pray for them regularly? Get your family and friends, your Sunday school and children's club involved, too. You can get more information from the Adopt-A-People Clearing House, 721 N. Tejon, Colorado Springs, CO 80901.

2. Does your church support any missionaries? Ask for their addresses and write to them, pray for them, and send them birthday and Christmas cards. You will learn many interesting things about missionary work from their replies.

3. Write to the children of missionary families. Tell them about life in your own country and ask them to tell you what it is like to live in another country. Ask your friends in your Sunday School class to help you make a tape with singing and talking on it and send it to them. Ask them to make a tape for you in return.

4. Ask your parents if you may get a good map of the world to put on your bedroom wall. Mark on it the people and places you have learned about. If you have pictures of missionaries you have met, stick those on the map to show where they work and remember to pray for them regularly.

5. Read missionary biographies. There are many very interesting ones and some have been written specially for children. In these true stories you will read about the happy, difficult, and exciting things that have happened to missionaries in their work. You can get a list of many of these books from the Children's Missions Resource Center. You will find the address below.

6. Get to know children from your school who come from other countries. They often feel very lonely. Make friends with them and invite them to your house to play. They may ask what makes you and your family different, and you will be able to tell them about God's love. Their parents may allow them to go to Sunday school with you.

7. Many of the missionary agencies listed on pages 124 and 125 have interesting stories, books, and videos about exciting places and people. Ask your parents or Sunday school teachers to find out about them.

8. These are only a few ideas to help you get involved in missions right now. For more projects and ideas for yourself, your family, and Sunday school ask your parents or teacher to write to Children's Missions Resource Center, 1605 Elizabeth Street, Pasadena, CA 91104, USA. One exciting booklet they have is "52 Fun Things Your Family Can Do Together for Missions." This costs $1.00 plus $1.00 shipping.

SOME FACTS ABOUT THE PEOPLES IN THIS BOOK

People	Estimated number	Main religions	Main countries in which they live
Azeri	15,000,000	Atheist/Muslim	Azerbaijan (CIS, Iran)
Baluch	6,000,000	Muslim	Iran, Pakistan
Children of the streets	30,000,000	Roman Catholic	Latin America
Dogon	500,000	Animist/Muslim	Mali
Euskaldunak	2,300,000	Roman Catholic	France, Spain
Falasha	70,000	Jewish/Christian	Ethiopia, Israel
Gypsies	34,000,000	Animist/Christian	Worldwide
Herero	140,000	Animist/Christian	Botswana, Namibia
Irula	48,000	Animist/Hindu	India
Jolas	500,000	Animist/Muslim	Gambia, Senegal
Kurds	20,000,000	Muslim	Iran, Iraq, Turkey
Lobi	340,000	Animist	Burkina Faso, Côte d'Ivoire
Minangkabau	6,500,000	Muslim	Indonesia
Navajo	200,000	Animist/Christian	United States
Ovambo	990,000	Animist/Christian	Namibia
Parsees	179,000	Zoroastrian	India – Bombay City
Quechua	13,000,000	Animist/Roman Catholic	Ecuador, Peru
Riff	1,500,000	Muslim	Morocco
San (Bushmen)	82,000	Animist	Botswana, Namibia
Tibetans	5,000,000	Buddhist	China
Uzbek	15,000,000	Muslim/Atheist	USSR, Afghanistan etc.
Vagla	10,000	Animist	Ghana
Wolof	2,600,000	Muslim, Animist	Senegal, Gambia etc.
Xhosa	6,700,000	Animist/Christian	South Africa
Yao	714,000	Animist	China, Thailand, Laos
Zulu	6,820,000	Animist/Christian	South Africa

MORE FACTS
about the countries in this book
including the countries from which the peoples in the book come.

Country	Main religious groups	Number of people	Area in square km
Albania	Atheist	3,300,000	29,000
Bhutan	Buddhist	700,000	47,000
Botswana	Animist	1,400,000	581,000
Burkina Faso	Animist/Muslim/Christian	9,600,000	274,000
Chad	Muslim/Christian	5,200,000	1,284,000
CIS (Ex USSR)	Atheist/Muslim/Christian	284,300,000	22,402,000
Djibouti	Muslim	400,000	23,000
Ethiopia	Coptic/Muslim	54,300,000	1,222,000
Fiji	Christian/Hindu	800,000	18,000
Gambia	Animist/Muslim	900,000	11,000
Ghana	Animist/Christian	16,000,000	238,000
Greece	Greek Orthodox	10,300,000	133,000
Haiti	Roman Catholic/Voodoo	6,400,000	28,000
India	Hindu/Muslim/Animist	882,600,000	3,204,000
Indonesia	Muslim/Christian	184,500,000	1,919,000
Israel	Jewish	5,200,000	21,000
Japan	Shinto/Buddhist	124,400,000	373,000
Korea (South)	Buddhist/Christian	44,300,000	99,000
Lesotho	Roman Catholic	1,900,000	30,000
Mali	Muslim	8,500,000	1,240,000
Mongolia	Atheist/Buddhist	2,300,000	1,565,000
Morocco	Muslim	26,000,000	447,000

Country	Main religions	Number of people	Area in square km
Namibia	Animist/Christian	1,500,000	823,000
New Zealand	Christian	3,400,000	268,000
Oman	Muslim	1,600,000	212,000
Pakistan	Muslim	121,700,000	804,000
Papua New Guinea	Christian	3,900,000	462,000
Peru	Roman Catholic	22,500,000	1,285,000
Qatar	Muslim	500,000	11,000
Romania	Orthodox Christian	23,200,000	237,000
Senegal	Animist/Muslim	7,900,000	196,000
South Africa	Animist/Christian	41,700,000	1,222,000
Spain	Roman Catholic	38,600,000	505,000
Sri Lanka	Buddhist	17,600,000	66,000
Thailand	Buddhist	56,300,000	514,000
Tibet – China	Buddhist	2,196,000	9,573,000
Turkey	Muslim	99,200,000	781,000
United Arab Emirates	Muslim	2,500,000	84,000
United States of America	Christian	255,600,000	9,373,000
Venezuela	Roman Catholic	18,900,000	912,000
Western Samoa	Christian	200,000	3,000
Xinjiang – China	Muslim	15,156,000	1,647,000
Yemen	Muslim	10,400,000	532,000
Zimbabwe	Christian/Animist	10,300,000	391,000

The population totals, with the exception of those for Tibet and Xinjiang, have been taken from the World Population Data Sheet (1992) of the Population Reference Bureau, Inc.

CHRISTIAN AGENCIES WHO WILL SEND YOU MORE INFORMATION ON REQUEST

People	Christian Agency	Country	Christian Agency
Azeri	WEC YWAM	Albania	Parl IPHM YWAM
Baluch	IVS WBT WEC	Bhutan	LM YWAM
Children	CBFM CMA Parl TEAM	Chad	MAF TEAM WBT WEC
Dogon	WBT	Djibouti	RSMT
Euskaldunak	EURO	Ethiopia	Parl
Falasha	SIM	Fiji	WEC YWAM
Gypsies	EURO	Greece	BCU
Herero	AIM MAF	Haiti	IPHM WGM OMS
Irula		Indonesia	CBFM CMA Parl TEAM
Jola	WEC	Japan	CBFM CMA Parl WGM
Kurds	WBT WEC	Korea (South)	OMS CMA KACWM TEAM
Lobi	WBT WEC	Lesotho	AIM APHM
Minangkabau	IMF OMF	Mongolia	MAF TEAM WEC
Navajo	WBT NGM	New Zealand	YWAM
Ovambo		Oman	AWM
Parsees	IS	Papua New Guinea	CMA WBT YWAM
Quecha	CMA Parl WBT	Qatar	
Riff		Romania	IPHM Parl TEAM
San (Bushmen)	MAF YWAM	Sri Lanka	Parl TEAM WEC
Tibetans	WEC TEAM	Turkey	Parl TEAM
Uzbek	WEC	United Arab Emirates	TEAM WEC
Vagla	WBT WEC	Venezuela	CBFM CMA TEAM
Wolof	SIM WBT WEC	Western Samoa	MCOD
Xhosa		Xinjiang-China	Parl WEC
Yao	Parl OMF	Yemen	
Zulu	Parl TEAM	Zimbabwe	Parl TEAM

On the next page you will find the addresses of all the agencies listed on this page. If you need more information about a country or a people group then write to the organization listed. Many will be able to help you, but not all of them will have materials specially prepared for children and young people.

ADDRESS LIST

AIM
Africa Inland Mission International Inc.
P.O. Box 178,
Pearl River, NY 10965

AWM
Arab World Ministries
P.O. Box 96,
Upper Darby, PA 19082

BCU
Bible Christian Union Inc.
P.O Box 410,
Hatfield, PA 19440-0410

CBFM
Conservative Baptist Foreign Mission Society
P.O. Box 5,
Wheaton, IL 60189-0005

CMA
Christian and Missionary Alliance
P.O. Box 35000,
Colorado Springs,
CO 80935-3500

EURO
Euromission,
Postbus 32,
3950 AC Maarn,
The Netherlands

FRO
Frontiers
325 North Stapley Drive,
Mesa, AZ 85203

IMF
Indonesian Missionary Fellowship
P.O. Box 4, Batu 65301,
E.Java, Indonesia

IS
Interserve
239 Fairfield Ave.,
P.O. Box 418,
Upper Darby, PA 19082

IVS
Mr. Irving Sylvia
18134 Woodbarn Lane,
Fountain Valley,
CA 92708

IPHM
International Pentecostal Holiness Church
World Missions Dept.,
P.O. Box 12609,
Oklahoma City,
OK 73157

KACWM
Korean American Society for World Mission
1605 Elizabeth St.,
Pasadena, CA 91104

LM
Leprosy Mission Int.
Goldhay Way,
Orton Goldhay,
Peterborough,
PE2 OGZ,
England

MAF
Mission Aviation Fellowship
P.O. Box 3202,
Redlands, CA 92373

MCOD
Methodist Church Overseas Division
25 Marylebone Road,
London NW1 5JR,
England

NGM
Navajo Gospel Mission
P.O. Box 3717,
Flagstaff, AZ 86003

OMF
Overseas Missionary Fellowship
404 S. Church St.,
Robesonia, PA 19551

OMS
OMS International
P.O. Box A,
Greenwood, IN 46142

ParI
Partners International,
P.O. Box 15025,
San Jose, CA 95115-0025

RSMT
Red Sea Mission Team
P.O. Box 16227,
Minneapolis, MN 55416

SIM
Society for International Ministries
P.O. Box 7900,
Charlotte, NC 28241

TEAM
The Evangelical Alliance Mission
P.O. Box 969,
Wheaton, IL 60189-0969

WBT
Wycliffe Bible Translators International
7500 West Camp Wisdom Road,
Dallas, TX 75326,

WEC
WEC International
P.O. Box 1707,
Fort Washington,
PA 19034-8707

WGM
World Gospel Mission
P.O. Box WGM,
Marion, IN 46952

YWAM
Youth With a Mission
P.O. Box 55309,
Seattle, WA 98155

ACKNOWLEDGMENTS

Many people and mission agencies have helped in the production of this book. They are too many to list, but to each one who patiently answered our many questions and provided valuable information and pictures, we give our grateful and heartfelt thanks. Our thanks are also due to those who have carefully checked the material and the facts and figures.

Jill drew much of the material for this book from the information gathered for the preparation of *Operation World*, the world prayer manual researched and written by her husband, Patrick. The new edition of *Operation World* is being published at the same time as *You Can Change the World*.

Others, through their letters and prayers, have been a constant source of inspiration and strength. Jill frequently expressed her appreciation of all who encouraged her as she sought to convey some of her own prayer concerns for this world and its people, firmly believing that children and young people have a vital role in changing the world through prayer. Before she was called to be with Jesus in heaven, the Lord gave Jill the strength to complete the text of the book. This gave her a great sense of joy, although it had been her desire to see the book published and being used by children and young people.

Shortly before her death Jill asked Daphne Spraggett, a friend and colleague in WEC International, to look after the revision and checking of the manuscript. Daphne has counted this a great privilege and is grateful to the many who have helped her in this task.

Copyright © 1992 Jill Johnstone
Design copyright © Three's Company 1993
First published in the United States by Zondervan Publishing House, 5300 Patterson Avenue, S.E., Grand Rapids, Michigan 49530
ISBN 0–310–40041–4
Reprinted 1994

Created by Three's Company, 12 Flitcroft Street, London WC2H 8DJ

Worldwide coedition organized and produced by Angus Hudson Ltd, Concorde House, Grenville Place, Mill Hill, London NW7 3SA

Illustrations by Tony Kenyon and Mary Filidis

Printed in Singapore

Enquiries from publishers relating to this title should be addressed to: Angus Hudson Ltd, Concorde House, Grenville Place, Mill Hill, London NW7 3SA, England. Telephone +44 81 959 3668. Facsimile +44 81 959 3678.